"Sheri Rose Shepherd is a leading voice for women today, an authority on all matters of the heart."

—KAREN KINGSBURY, *New York Times* bestselling novelist

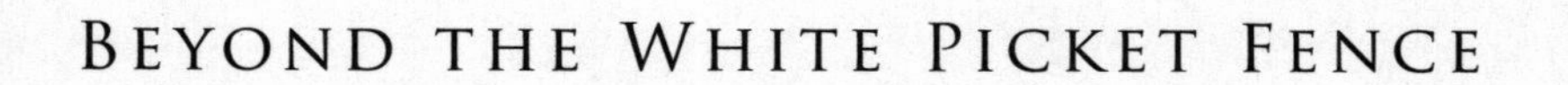

Beyond the White Picket Fence

BEYOND THE *White Picket Fence*

WHAT TO DO WHEN YOUR LIFE IS DISMANTLED

AWARD-WINNING AUTHOR

SHERI ROSE SHEPHERD

an imprint of Regnery Publishing
Washington, D.C.

ISBN: 978-1-68451-028-3
eISBN: 978-1-68451-144-0

Library of Congress Control Number: 2020945136

Published in the United States by
Salem Books
An Imprint of Regnery Publishing
A Division of Salem Media Group
Washington, D.C.
www.SalemBooks.com

Manufactured in the United States of America

10 9 8 7 6 5 4 3 2 1

Contents

Introduction

The Dismantling of My Life

Dear Sister in Christ,

I know how hard it is when you're right in the middle of a devastating dismantling season of life to even believe you can come up for air, let alone find the strength to build. In part, this book is meant to get you healed so that you can become even stronger in your faith, your emotions, and your reactions. My purpose in writing this book is to show you your God-given right to rise up from the ashes and become a beautiful representation of His glorious grace and prove our wounds can work for us as God's power and promise are displayed in devastation.

I'll never forget the night my dad came into my room after another exasperating fight with my mom. I saw the fear on his face and the tears in his eyes as he knelt by my bed to tell me he was moving out. I love my dad so much, and he loved his family. But he didn't know how to save us at the time. I hugged him tightly as I felt my heart shattering. I knew that everything in my life was about to shift, and there was nothing I could do about it. I was only eleven years old. When I was young, I didn't know anybody with divorced parents, so I processed my pain by myself, and I felt so alone.

Little did I know that God would one day use my childhood devastation to help heal broken hearts and restore faith foundations. I did not know the Lord then. Actually, I was Jewish. I didn't give my life to Jesus until my twenty-fourth birthday, a night when I had planned on taking my own life. I called on the name of Jesus, and He truly saved me from myself and from my sin.

Sadly, I lost my Jewish family for my faith in Jesus and once again walked my journey alone. It was ten years before things changed. It was hard to live out my faith with their disapproval, but today my entire Jewish family knows the Lord!

To be honest, I was sure that my faithfulness to God, my decision to marry a Christian man, and my commitment to full-time ministry ensured me a life where the enemy couldn't destroy my family foundation. But five years ago, my life was dismantled in every way. I lost everything I loved all at once. And I am not going to lie—it was devastating, and I definitely wondered where God was and why this was happening to me when I had been faithful in serving Him for twenty-five years. The book of Job describes my life all the way down to the boils on Job's skin. My boils have come in the form of cancerous tumors all over my lymphatic system. Job 19:13–14 says, "My relatives stay far away, and my friends have turned against me. My family is gone, and my close friends have forgotten me."

While I don't want to share the devil's details or dishonor those involved, I do want to share with you how God can use our devastation to do new things. Mistakes can be our tutors, and our pain can give us the passion we need to pursue our God-given purposes. When we go through trials, God gives us empathy and compassion for the people He brings across our path. In our trials, we come to understand things that never would have been revealed to us without that refining work.

With the help of the Holy Spirit, I made hard and heartbreaking choices to reverse the curse of the enemy's work in my life. I started with the first foundation that was destroyed, which was my marriage. After our divorce, my ex-husband and I decided to forgive ourselves and each other for the wrong and hurtful things we did to each other during our twenty-five-year marriage. My ex-husband is now remarried to someone else, and I have chosen to remain single (unless God sends me a surprise). Right now, I am content right where I am. As weird as this sounds, I actually like the woman Steve married. (It helps that she had nothing to do with our marriage ending.)

Since then, Steve and I have made peace so that we don't add any more heartache to our adult children's lives than our divorce already has. Our hope is that God's mercy and grace can be seen through our intentional action. Yes, God hates divorce—*not* because He is mad at us, but because He knows the pain that happens when our hearts and vows are broken and the family foundation He built for us is dismantled.

Right now, you may be thinking, "Sheri Rose, you have no idea what I have been through." You're right—I don't, and I never want to underestimate anyone's pain. But I do know what it feels like to be so heartbroken and horrified by what happened to your life that you think you're never going to come up again for air. I am living proof that there is life after the death of everything you love. There is life beyond the devastation of the white picket fence. It may not be the life you envisioned, but God is the master of remodeling the ruins if we make room for Him in our hearts and in our homes. Because I am fighting cancer, I have a continual reminder of how precious each day is. I praise the Lord that He helped me to process my pain. In exchange, I choose to take His new beginning, not looking back, so I can live out the call of God on my life, one day at time.

I know it seems impossible to believe that just one person's right reaction to the ruins could help to rebuild, repair, or redeem anything out of the wreckage in this world. King David was one person with enough faith to kill a giant that everyone else was afraid to face. Queen Esther, an orphan, was one person who saved a nation. Nehemiah was one person who inspired God's people to help rebuild the broken city walls that the enemy had destroyed. That broken wall was like a white picket fence that represented the protection of that city. God didn't even give them new materials to build from. Instead, He showed them how He could take the broken pieces and rebuild. Eventually, that wall became stronger than the original, but not without a fight.

With that said, would you consider taking a step of faith by putting purpose to your pain by using the broken pieces of your past—or present—to lay a new faith foundation for our future generations to stand on long after you're gone?

Love,

Sheri Rose

"They will rebuild the ancient ruins, repairing cities destroyed long ago. They will revive them, though they have been deserted for many generations." (Isaiah 61:4)

The War Story behind the White Picket Fence

Most people don't know that the white picket fence was not created to represent the dream life it is known for today. On the contrary, its origin arose from the pain and sacrifice of contributing to the war effort in World War II. During the 1940s, our military was running out of ammunition. In order to keep up the good fight, Americans dismantled their wrought-iron fences and gave them to the military. The iron was then melted down, reformed, and given to our soldiers to use as ammunition to defeat our enemy. Once a family dismantled their iron fence, they put up a white picket fence to replace it. The white picket fence soon came to represent the family's willingness to give up whatever they had to in order to fight for our freedoms. It's amazing what we can do when we have the right ammunition to fight for the things worth fighting for!

Many of us all over the world have had our lives dismantled by the enemy of our soul. Right now, you may even feel like there is nothing left worth fighting for. This beautiful battle book will open your eyes so you can see with an eternal view of what God can do with the broken pieces of our lives if we work with Him. Each story is based in truth, but I have changed the names and some details to protect those in each story.

Get ready to be engaged, empowered, encouraged, and educated on how to use whatever you have walked through to make an everlasting impact that will echo throughout all eternity.

Chapter 1

Beyond Betrayal

GOD, HELP ME TO RISE UP, REDEEM, AND REBUILD FROM THE RUINS OF MY LIFE.

Kevin and Marie were college sweethearts who dreamed of furthering God's Kingdom together. They knew God had brought them together for more than a "happily ever after." They both had a God-given dream to do something with a greater purpose than living for themselves, so they dedicated their marriage to the ministry of pastoring a church. They were passionate people and were always about doing their Heavenly Father's business. Kevin and Marie were the kind of couple everyone admired because of their love for each other; it was evident that their marriage had a great purpose.

During the first decade of their marriage and ministry, God blessed them with a growing church, two beautiful children, and a strong love for each other. They were an extremely generous couple who had beautiful hearts for humanity. The governor of their home state even presented them with a humanitarian award for the positive changes they brought about in their city.

One day, a young lady burst through the door of the church office. She was crying hysterically. Kevin heard her and came out of his office to see what he might do to help. As she struggled to catch her breath, she told him about her desperate attempts to escape from her abusive husband. But every time she tried to leave, he talked her into coming back. He would change his ways and be kind for about a month, but then the cycle of abuse towards her and the children would start again, growing more severe each time. She was scared and felt completely helpless.

"I'm not religious and I'm not a Christian, but I heard this church helps people who are hurting and in need of help," she said, "so this is where I came."

Kevin quickly called Marie and asked if she could come to the church to help this woman and her children. Marie's heart broke for the woman—Miranda—and she immediately got in the car and came to the rescue. As soon as Marie arrived, she hugged the woman, helped her and her kids gather some clothes from the church's closet, and then took them to her home to spend the night. Miranda's kids were four and six years old, and Kevin and Marie's children were teenagers. Kevin and Marie's kids were sweet and helpful with the young children while their parents ministered to Miranda together.

That night, when Kevin and Marie were in bed, Marie rolled over to face Kevin and said, "Why don't we have Miranda and her children stay with us for the next month so they have some stability? They need a spiritual family and a safe place to heal." Kevin agreed.

Each evening, Marie would make dinner for everyone. They would sit around the table together and play board games. They laughed together and talked about the Lord daily. Kevin and Marie would pray together each night for Miranda and her children to come to know the Lord. Within a week, their prayers were answered. Miranda asked for prayer to receive Jesus as her Savior, and then the kids said they wanted to receive Jesus too. It was a glorious night, and they celebrated by taking communion together.

A couple of weeks later, Miranda's kids started asking questions like "Pastor Kevin, can I call you Daddy since I don't have a daddy anymore?" Miranda also began saying things like "I want to have a marriage exactly like yours one day." She asked Kevin and Marie to pray for her to meet a man who would love her and her children the way that Kevin loved Marie and their children. They felt satisfied that they had done the work of the Lord in her life. They knew they had set a great example of what a family should look like for her and her children.

As time went on, four weeks turned into three months, and some of Kevin's trusted friends could see that Miranda was beginning to get too attached to him and Marie. One of the elders pulled Kevin aside after church. "I believe Miranda could easily become attracted to you if she stays in your home any longer. She is continually talking about what an amazing marriage you have and how she wants to have a husband just like you. I think it's time for you and Marie to move her into a home where she can be with another single mom in the church."

The next night, while Pastor Kevin was hosting a men's Bible study in his home, some of the other men also said they felt it was not good for Miranda and her children to stay there any longer. They told him it was imperative to move her out that week and promised to help gather more support around her to keep her company as the transition took place.

But Pastor Kevin told them, "Marie and I are really helping her. I can't ask her to leave now; she has become spiritual family to us, and we have really grown to love her and her children." Even though his trusted friends and elders were persistent, Kevin defended himself and denied their wisdom. Honestly, Kevin loved his wife very much and was in no way attracted to Miranda, so he truly thought he was doing the right thing.

That night when Kevin and Marie were in bed, he told Marie what the elders had said. Marie replied, "Maybe they're right." Marie also had grown to love Miranda and her children, and she cried at the thought of their moving out. But then she thought about the elders and their godly friends' words; she trusted them so much. "Kevin, maybe we should listen to their wisdom and help her get started on a new life on her own."

"Marie, what if her ex-husband finds her and hurts her and the children? Plus, our kids are helping her kids so much, and they adore them. They'd be heartbroken if they left now!" he responded convincingly.

Marie trusted Kevin's pure heart. Even though she had a check in her spirit, she followed his lead because she really loved Miranda and her kids.

The next night, while Marie and the kids were at Vacation Bible School, Kevin was home alone with Miranda. She walked into his office while he was working on his sermon for Sunday and asked him to pray for her.

"Of course. What do you need me to pray for?" he asked.

"I have fallen in love with a married man at our church, and I need God to help me walk away," she replied.

Pastor Kevin was shocked. "Who could that possibly be, Miranda? You've been with us the whole time."

She replied by sitting in his lap and kissing his forehead. He tried to push her away, but she persisted, and eventually temptation took him over. In a moment of weakness, he actually ended up sleeping with Miranda that night. When they were done, Kevin sent her out to her room.

Kevin was sick in his spirit when Marie and all the kids came home. She could see something was wrong, but in her wildest dreams she never would have believed Kevin could cheat on her.

"I need to talk with you right now," he said desperately. "Can we go outside?"

Marie began to pray quietly. They stepped outside, and Kevin closed the door. He grabbed Marie, held her tightly, began crying uncontrollably, and told her what had happened.

Marie was mortified and cried out hysterically, "Kevin, how did this happen? If only we had listened to the warnings! What are we going to do?"

Kevin knew this was more than either of them could handle alone, so he immediately called one of the elders, who was like a spiritual father for him and Marie. They let him know what had happened, and he came over immediately to meet with them.

Meanwhile, another woman from the church took Miranda and her children to her home. The youth pastor came over to sit with Kevin and Marie's teenage children while they tried to sort through the crisis that night.

Over the next several weeks, Kevin had someone else run the church's weekend services. Kevin and Marie's family worked with professional counselors. He desperately wanted to put the broken pieces of their family back together. But every time he looked at his children or Marie, he could only see them through the filter of his failure. He couldn't forgive himself, even though God and his wife had already forgiven him. Sadly, he bowed down to Satan's ultimate plan, and he left Marie and their children.

Kevin convinced himself that he was not worthy of God's forgiveness and mercy. Kevin went into hiding for weeks; Marie and their children had no idea where he was. Sadly, Kevin reached out to Miranda, and they began to see each other in secret. Eventually, he moved in with her and her children.

Tragically, everything Kevin and Marie had built was dismantled. There Marie was without her husband and without a ministry. Suddenly, she was a single mom trying to explain to her teenage children how this had happened. This was the most heart-wrenching thing she had ever experienced. She felt helpless and hopeless. All she could think about was how she and Kevin had reached out to help a single mom, and now she was the single mom without her husband and the father of her children.

Over and over, Marie replayed the conversation she'd had with Kevin the night before it had happened. She struggled to forgive herself for not taking the advice to move Miranda out. Marie was afraid that her children would blame God, so she kept reminding them, “This was not God’s will; it was the fall of your father in a weak moment.”

Over the next few years, Marie tried to repair the shattered pieces of her life. She kept begging God for her children not to fall away from Him because of what their father had done. She continued to say to herself, “I must keep following God, and He will get us through this.” She held on to Christian friends who loved her no matter what she was going through or how hard her life got. She clung to the people who had grace for her throughout the healing process. The life she had always known was dedicated to the ministry God gave her, and now she was the one who so desperately needed ministry.

Two years after Kevin’s exit, he was still living with Miranda and her children, but they were not married. One day, during a routine medical check-up, he was diagnosed with acute leukemia and given ten weeks to live. Miranda, who was still in her early thirties, decided she did not want to take care of a dying older man. She forged his signature on a check, emptied his bank account, took her kids, and left him alone to die. Then she disappeared, never to be heard from again.

Kevin had no wife, no family, and no loving church body to rally around him. In fact, he had nothing to show for his years of hard work and dedication to his ministry. During that time in Kevin’s life, Marie was shopping at a grocery store when a friend approached her and said, “Have you heard the news about Kevin?”

She told Marie that Kevin had been given a fatal diagnosis and Miranda had left him to die.

Marie had every reason to never talk to Kevin again. She had every reason to sit back and watch him pay the price for what his sin had cost all of them. But something deep down inside her wanted redemption more than revenge. She made the extremely hard decision to let go of her feelings and to look at the bigger picture of the legacy she wanted her children to see: she chose to love Kevin most when he deserved it the least for the sake of God's being glorified.

With her mind made up, she told her children and her friends that she was going to visit Kevin at the hospital and take care of him until his dying day. Her friends all begged her not to go because they didn't want to see her heart break even more. But Marie was convinced that despite all he had done to wrong her, Kevin should not die alone.

You can imagine how Kevin felt when Marie walked into his hospital room and looked into his eyes. She was not gloating with condemnation; instead, she offered to care for and love him. That one act of obedience began to heal Marie's heart from the horrific betrayal and embarrassment she had suffered.

But her friends, family, and even her children were angry at her for doing what she felt was right in God's sight. They saw Kevin's sin and the pain it had caused, and in their own pain, they wanted to react with what Kevin deserved. Marie's church and children asked her why she was helping Kevin after all the damage he had done. She knew her friends were thinking of her broken heart, and she was grateful that they loved her so much. But she also knew that even in Jesus's most painful moments, He was able to forgive and extend love in a way that changed people's lives and eternities.

Marie spent every one of Kevin's last days and nights with him at the hospital. She never left his side. There was a lot of reflecting and reminiscing. They even got to a point where they could laugh at some of the things they had done together when they were in love. With each laugh, Kevin would grab Marie's hand and kiss it as he looked in her eyes and cried tears of remorse. Marie received more healing every day that she shared with him.

One day after Kevin reached out to hold her hand, he slipped into a comatose state. Marie cried out for the nurses to help her, and she cried out to God while she waited for them to arrive. She knew in her heart that Kevin was in his final hours and would soon be home with the Lord.

Marie wanted her children and her church to somehow experience the closure she was experiencing before Kevin went home to be with the Lord. She quickly called them to ask if they would join her in her final hours with Kevin.

Marie's family and church had struggled, but they loved Marie and decided to honor her wishes even though they disagreed with her actions. When they arrived, they found Marie kneeling by Kevin's bed. She had his favorite worship music playing, and the room was filled with peace. Once everyone was there, Marie asked everyone to grab hands and circle around Kevin's bed. Then she asked if anyone would be willing to share a story of how Kevin had touched their life when he was their pastor.

At first, the room was quiet, and then one of Kevin's old friends broke the silence. This began a series of beautiful stories, remembering the parts of Kevin's life that were lived so well for others. Even though Kevin could not respond, they knew he could hear their voices because tears began to flood his pillow. As each person shared their story of the work God had done through him, Marie glanced over to see her children begin to break as well.

God was glorified as redeeming love flowed out through the healing power of forgiveness. The biggest blessing for Marie was watching both her children walk over to kiss their father's forehead. For the rest of their time together that day, each of her children held one of Kevin's hands. Marie's mama's heart wept tears of thanksgiving because that was the first time her children had loved on their father since he left them. She understood the significance of that moment, as this would be the last time they had a chance to do so.

Marie could see that God was doing a great work as they began to speak of the good father their dad had been to them when they were growing up. Even more beautiful was when she got to see her own obedience bring an outcome that never would've happened if she didn't let the Holy Spirit lead her to this moment. As they held their father's hands and tears flowed down her children's cheeks, Marie could see their Heavenly Father holding them and healing their hearts.

Finally, Marie asked if everybody would leave the room and pray outside. When they were gone, she got in the hospital bed, held her husband, and whispered in his ear, "I will always love you, and

I will never forget the beautiful life we had together. I will see you in Heaven one day, and we will celebrate this redeeming moment and all the faith adventures we shared together."

She felt him squeeze her hand as he drew his final breath. Her heart was filled with the peace and the pain of saying goodbye. As her tears joined his on his pillow, Marie felt the Holy Spirit holding her as she held her husband for the last time.

What Can God Do?

Today, Kevin's son Mark is the pastor of the church Kevin and Marie started as a young couple. Many former members have returned, and now their church is even stronger and more effective in that community than before. God proves His redemption is always possible.

It may not look the same in your story because our sins and our circumstances are all different. But isn't it amazing that our God is so gracious and so invested in our furthering His Kingdom on Earth that, even though Kevin fell, his many years of ministry and his faith foundation live on through his son, daughter, and grandchildren? They all can live free of regret, anger, and bitterness because they chose to honor their mom and say a final goodbye to their father in a setting of God's glorious love. Marie deactivated the devil's work her husband's sin had brought into their family. She was determined not to waste the devastation. Her extraordinary act of obedience changed her children's future and the future of their church forever—even if it had to take place on Kevin's deathbed after their marriage ended.

FYI: God sent Marie an amazing new husband who was a widower and former pastor. He loved and adored her. They laughed a lot and loved each other and others well. Her new husband, Jim, became a precious grandfather for her grandchildren, and they spent twenty faith-filled, adventurous years in full-time missions ministry, traveling the world together.

WHAT CAN I DO?

Before I share what you can do, I want to say that if you've been betrayed, I am so sorry. My heart breaks with you because I know that kind of pain. The betrayal of someone you love and trust is awful. One thing I am careful of is never to "casualize" a casualty. When you are in the middle of crippling emotional pain, it's hard to believe you will ever breathe again. When someone you love betrays you, whether it's a grown child, a parent, or a spouse, the heartbreak is excruciating. When I was going through my four-year crisis, I stepped off the stage and stopped speaking and writing to give myself time to heal. I knew that if I could not breathe myself, there was no way I could help someone else put their "oxygen mask" on in that season of pain. I had to remember this, and I want you to remember it as well: God loves you, and He wants to take care of you. He wants to heal you, and He wants to help you through this. I know it's hard to push through pain, but it's even harder to know that you wasted it.

Give Yourself Freedom to Be Real and Heal

The Bible refers to God's emotions two thousand times, and you are created in His image. If you don't let yourself process your feelings, you will get stuck in your story of the betrayal. Make a list and identify everything you're feeling. I would encourage you to go to the Word and look up those feelings. But I'd also encourage you to process your feelings with a trustworthy friend who loves you, knows the Word, and will give you freedom to feel. Keep in mind that even Scripture can be used as a Band-Aid. You don't want to put a Band-Aid over a bleeding soul wound. The wound needs to air out by processing your feelings with a good friend or counselor. It's one thing for someone to tell you a Bible verse, but it's another thing for someone to use it as a healing balm for your hurting soul. This is not the time to be around people who speak "Christianese" but don't know how to be compassionate. With that said, let me offer a bit of caution: you want to walk with people who have wisdom and will let you have what I call "freak-out grace," but who also won't let you do anything you'll regret after you're healed.

Process with the Right People

During a healing time, it's very important that you disconnect from negative or insensitive people or those who do not have empathy for where you are in that moment. Even those with good intentions who love you can hinder your healing. It's OK to tell them you don't want to talk about something. It's also OK to get help from those who can actually help heal you. Honestly, when you're in the middle of an emotional or relational crisis, you really need people who will just listen and serve silently.

During your healing season, pay close attention to how you feel after people leave. Do you feel closer to God? Do you feel stronger? Do you feel comforted? When I was going through my four-year healing crisis, I learned it was better for me to be alone with the Lord than to be with the wrong people. Remember that some people don't mean any harm and don't mean to hurt you while you're already hurting—they've just never been where you've been, and they have no idea how to handle your heart. But whatever the reason, this is your season to get healed.

Exchange Bitterness for a Better Outcome

What if Marie had decided to hold on to bitterness and let Kevin die alone? It would've been a very different outcome to this God story. Marie's church never would've gotten to see what it looks like to live out the legacy of forgiveness. Her children never would have had a chance to say goodbye to their father. Kevin would've died alone, feeling like a failure. Marie would not have had the chance to get the true healing for her heart that only comes by extraordinary acts of love and forgiveness. I was even thinking about the nurses and the doctors coming in and out of the room who knew the story. I wonder how many of them got to witness what faith is really for and who Christ really is when it comes to a crisis situation like that. Honestly, when you're hurting, it's not easy—"Revenge feels good for a moment, but a right reaction brings redemption that lasts a lifetime."

Marie is a hero of the faith—not because she's better than any of us, but because she made the hard decision to do something extraordinary. She did not let her emotions direct her decisions. She was even able to recognize that the emotions of other people who had been hurt were keeping them from forgiving Kevin and keeping them trapped in their unforgiveness. Yes, she was heartbroken, but she decided to make her faith more important than her feelings, and she got to see the amazing fruits of her obedient choice.

His Love Letter to You

Beloved Child,

I see you when you are in the garden of grief, My princess. I hear your cry for help in the dark hours of the night. I Myself cried out in the garden the night I was betrayed. In My suffering, I asked My Father for another way—a less painful way. Yet I trusted His will and purpose for My life. I knew the ultimate victory was at the cross. Just as olives must be crushed to make oil, I poured out My life as a love offering for you. Don't ever doubt that I am with you and that I long to take you to a place of comfort, peace, and victory. Even when you cannot see Me from where you are, I am working on your behalf. Give to Me the crushing weight of your circumstances, and come to Me in prayer. When it is time to leave the garden, I will walk with you across the valley and straight to the cross—where your trials will be transformed into triumph.

Love,

Your Savior who loves you with His life!

"All praise to God, the Father of our Lord Jesus Christ. God is our merciful Father and the source of all comfort. He comforts us in all our troubles so that we can comfort others. When they are troubled, we will be able to give them the same comfort God has given us." (2 Corinthians 1:3–4)

Chapter 2

BEYOND FORGIVENESS

GOD, SHOW ME HOW TO FORGIVE WHAT I CAN'T FORGET SO THAT I CAN MOVE FORWARD INTO THE FUTURE YOU HAVE FOR ME.

My mom, Carole, grew up in a home without any love whatsoever. Her mom, my grandma, wouldn't even let me call her "Grandma." I've never had a hug from either of them.

My mom's parents believed that kids should be seen but never heard. As a young girl, my mother wasn't allowed to sit at the dinner table with them during meals. She never felt the love of a mother tucking her into bed or telling her how special she was before she fell asleep. She was never allowed to have friends over to play with at home. In fact, she was never really allowed to be a child.

Carole's parents bought a little table that they put in the corner of their dining room where she would eat every day alone in silence. Her only friends were the ones she made up in her mind. She created make-believe stories that she grew up believing, and soon she was unable to tell the difference between make-believe and reality.

When she was a teenager, Carole attended Hollywood High School in Southern California. One day, a television producer came to audition kids for a singing group on the local TV station, and she decided to try out. She thought maybe this was her big breakthrough to fame and the finances she desperately needed to get out of her horrific situation at home.

That day, my mom discovered she had a beautiful voice, and she was given the lead position in the group. I'm sure it helped that she was absolutely physically gorgeous. The production team asked her to stop by the TV station after school because they felt she was a potential star, and they wanted to strike a contract with her. They only needed one thing to move forward: her parents' signatures.

She thought up a lie quickly: "Um...my parents are both gone for the week, so how about this? I'll take the papers home and make sure they sign them as soon as they get back." The producers agreed, and she was off. She forged both parents' signatures and mailed them to the station, thinking that would make it look more official. Next, she lied to her parents and told them she had to stay after school for mandatory study groups, but in reality, she was at the TV station for rehearsals.

One night, her mom and dad happened to be flipping through the only five TV channels they had back then and saw my mom on the TV show. They freaked out because somehow she had broken out of their prison of solitude and isolation. Her dad went into her room, hit her in the face, and screamed at her that they would kick her out onto the streets if she didn't quit the show and sue the TV station because she was only fifteen.

Carole was devastated. She desperately began begging her dad in tears, "Please, Father, don't take this from me! You've taken everything from me!" His only response was another punch, and the beating continued.

When she went to bed that night, instead of falling into a deep sleep, she fell into a deep dark hole of depression. Every day, she wanted to die. (Even when I was a little girl, she would threaten to kill herself weekly by putting a razor blade to her wrist. I would scream and beg her not to do it. I was terrified that unless I was the perfect child or the perfect counselor who listened to all her issues, she would take her life.)

The next morning, her dad physically picked her up, threw her into the car, and drove her down to the TV station. He dragged her in and demanded to see the producer in charge immediately. He said he would sue the station for putting his minor daughter on TV and exposing her that way. She was hysterically crying, and her dad was screaming at the top of his lungs, "Take all the shows that she's in off the air now!"

The next three years of Carole's life were hell on earth. She couldn't wait until she was eighteen so she could break free from being beaten down emotionally and physically. When she wasn't being beaten, she was left completely alone. She withered inside, like a dried-out flower with nothing left to give. At school, she would sit in the corner, unsure of how to connect or communicate with girls her age. She had learned to flirt because that at least seemed to get attention from boys. She enjoyed it because it felt like love to her.

The day my mom turned eighteen, she went out and looked for any man who would marry her. She met someone that very night and married him a week later just to get out of her parents' home. Tragically, the man she married was just as abusive as her father. She decided to run away, but just when she was ready to do it, she found out she was pregnant with their first baby. When she gave birth, the baby was brain-damaged.

She hated her marriage, mothering, life, and she hated herself. The only way she found relief was getting dolled up and walking the streets where men fell over themselves to talk to her and tell her how beautiful she was. What started out as attention turned into an endless string of affairs.

Carole became a master of making herself both the star and the victim of every script she wrote in her mind. She eventually lost the ability to discern her real life from the lies she'd made up. She won a local beauty pageant, and she loved the drama of Hollywood.

My mom met my dad while she was married to her first husband. They had an affair, and she finally left her husband when she became pregnant with me. But no matter how much attention my mom got or how loved my dad tried to make her feel, she couldn't get past her pain. Instead, she stayed stuck in her story; she didn't know how to break free. Now that I'm an adult, I can look back and see how badly my mom was hurting when I was a child. But sadly, because she never dealt with her childhood traumas, she let history repeat itself, and she treated me like her mother had treated her.

All the things her mom had done that she resented, she did to me. One part of me hurt for her because she was crying all the time, and the other part of me was crying out for her to be the mom that I needed so badly. I went to bed crying most nights. I always wished I had a mom to tuck me in bed at night, read me a story, kiss me on the forehead, and tell me how special I was. But because she didn't like herself, she couldn't show love to me. As a result, I never heard the words "I'm proud of you" or "I love you."

She was physically beautiful, and I was an overweight little girl, so I felt very ugly in comparison. When I would have neighborhood friends over to play, she would always tell them how pretty they were, and then she would ask me in front of my them, "Sheri Rose, why can't you be thin and pretty like your friend?"

It hurt, but honestly, I was fat because I substituted food for the comfort I was craving from her. I could not control my overeating binges. When she wasn't comparing me, she was criticizing me. I was so desperate to connect with her that I would listen to anything she tried to share with me, even if it meant being her seven-year-old counselor. By age eleven, I was exasperated. I eventually gave up trying to get her attention or approval. I felt my heart completely shut down and disconnect to the point that not only could I no longer feel her feelings anymore, but I couldn't feel my own.

She was addicted to male attention. When my dad was working, she would take me out, drive to a local hotel, and leave me in the car while she met various men for secret affairs. Then she would tell me that she would kill herself if I said anything to my dad. When we walked in the door, she would effortlessly lie to him. "Oh, we were just out getting an ice cream cone. Isn't that right, Sheri Rose?"

I know she was messed up, but it was heartbreaking to be her daughter. My dad's was the only love I knew, and he was working all the time. But he always made sure he was accessible to me, and that really helped.

But eventually, my dad couldn't take the affairs and lying either. My parents divorced, and I was left alone with my mom for a very short season. I finally told the courts the truth about my situation, and God made a way for me to get away from her and move in with my dad, who ultimately raised me. I was so thankful to be with such a positive dad who loved me so much.

I had a few sporadic visits with my mom once I moved out, but she was so angry at me for moving in with my dad that they never went well. I only saw her five times, and each visit was worse than when I lived with her. She refused to connect with me, so we would just sit there in silence. When I would say goodbye and try to hug her, she would push me away. Eventually, she shut down and chose not to have a relationship with me at all. Ironically, no matter what she did or said to me or how much she cut me out, I couldn't get past my longing for my real mom to love me.

When I moved in with my dad, I was twelve years old. I became determined to find myself a stepmom for my dad to fall in love with. Maybe I could find someone who would love us both. At the time, my dad owned an advertising agency. He often visited different hotels for their marketing, and I got to go with him. At one particular hotel, a really sweet waitress named Susie was at the restaurant bar. I was playing by the pool while my dad had a business meeting, and she was bringing me fancy little drinks and talking so sweetly with me. I told her that I wanted her to go on a date with my dad that night. She just giggled and asked, "Who is your dad?"

I pointed to him. He was sitting at the restaurant bar, discussing a new marketing plan with the owner of the hotel. She walked over to him and said, "Your daughter set you and me up for a date tonight."

Ironically, her last name was the same as my dad's and mine. I was sure it was a done deal. We visited that hotel several times, and every time, I would make him go out on a date with Susie. Well, on the fifth date, it stuck, and they became an official couple. Susie started flying in to come see my dad and me almost every weekend. She was so wonderful to be with—she was everything I wanted in a mom. I kept begging my dad to marry her, and eventually, he did. Honestly, for a season it felt like things were "happily ever after."

Susie spoke life to me. She was not a Christian at the time, and neither was I. We were all Jewish.

A few years later, as I was entering my high school, I was at a party when some friends put LSD in my beer. It was a hallucinogen that made me feel crazy and out of control. I was so scared, and, as it turned out, it almost took my life. I was rushed to the hospital. I was so freaked out from the whole experience that I never wanted to party with my friends again. When my stepmom came into the hospital room, she compassionately confronted me, saying, "Sheri

Rose, how long are you going to use your past and the pain with your mom as an excuse to self-destruct? If you will let me, I will help you."

I knew I needed help, so I agreed. She helped me lose over fifty pounds, encouraged me to stop hanging out with the wrong friends, and taught me how to take care of myself for the first time in my life. She changed everything about me—or, I should say, she inspired me to become the best version of myself.

During my senior year of high school, Susie entered me in a beauty pageant. I had never been on a runway before, so with that intensely bright spotlight in front of me, I actually walked off the end of the platform and fell onto the judges' table because I was blinded by it. I've always been somewhat quick-witted, so instead of wallowing, I hopped to my feet with my ripped-up evening gown and hurting hip and quickly exclaimed, "I just wanted to make sure you remembered me!"

Everybody started cracking up as I dragged myself backstage. And yes, the judges remembered me. I actually won the beauty pageant that night. They told me they wouldn't have picked me to win, but the way I reacted to the fall changed their vote. Somehow, those judges' words made me realize that the way I chose to react to things would determine the way my life turned out—for better or for worse.

Sadly, shortly after that, my stepmom took a bad turn herself. She emptied my dad's bank account and left us both. I was once again without a mom, and everything I thought I had was suddenly gone again. When I was in my twenties, I think my experience with

Susie and my mom really hit me hard. I'd begun having lots of worldly success, so on the outside, it appeared I had the world on a string, but on the inside, I was dying and desperate for the love of a mom. I think my dad was so disillusioned by two women in a row breaking his heart that a part of him also was dying inside. He still did his best to be the most positive dad he could be under the circumstances, but I could tell his heart was a wreck.

By age twenty-four, my inward pain had become overwhelming. I believe the enemy delivered the final blow when he deposited a thought in my head to take my own life.

I went to a doctor the next day and told him I was having trouble sleeping. I asked if he would prescribe some sleeping pills. I checked into a hotel room that night with the intention of taking my life. With the sleeping pills in my hand and desperation drowning my heart, I cried out, "Where are You, God? If You exist, show me!"

I fell asleep on the floor of that hotel with the sleeping pills still in my hand. The phone rang in the morning—a boyfriend asking if I would go to his grandparents' house with him that night for dinner. He mentioned that they were Christian missionaries. "Come on, Sheri Rose. They're very boring, so I need you to come with me and keep me company. You always know how to light up a room!" he said. I decided to join him.

That night, when I walked into the warm house, his grandmother, Emily, greeted me with a hug and asked if I wanted to go out to the garden with her to pick the ingredients for the salad she was making. I was mesmerized by her kind eyes, and she kept touching my back sweetly, as if to say, "Welcome to our home." She had set a beautiful table. I'd never sat around a dinner table with family growing up. My parents rarely had dinner together, and if they did, it was consumed by fighting. So being invited to sit at this table of love and peace was so healing.

Then Grandpa Charlie prayed for the meal. When he was done, he looked at his wife so adoringly. They'd been married for over fifty years, but his gaze made it seem like he was more in love with her now than when he first laid eyes on her. As I sat at dinner with this amazing couple, I was so intrigued by their humility, their obvious joy, and their pure hearts that I never wanted to leave their home. I found myself wishing I could stay there instead of the hotel.

Just then, Emily asked if I would like to check out of my hotel and spend the rest of the month at their home while I was in town producing a showcase. With tears in my eyes, I excitedly blurted out, "I would love it!"

My boyfriend looked at me, shocked. "What do you mean—you're going to stay here with my grandparents?"

I looked at him and said, "I absolutely want to stay here!"

My boyfriend took me to the hotel to get my stuff; he thought I was crazy. He took for granted the loving family that I wanted more than anything. But God really showed off that night when He gave me the one thing I'd always longed for as a child. Just as I settled into my new room, Emily came in and asked if she could tuck me into bed and read me a psalm from the Bible.

I'd asked God the night before if He existed. The following night, He gave me the deepest desire of my heart—being tucked in bed by a mom, being read to, and to top it all off, before she left the room, Emily kissed me on the forehead and said, "We're so glad you're here, Sheri Rose." I felt like I had finally found the mom I had been longing for all my life in this missionary grandmother.

I was beyond thankful. Every morning, I got to have breakfast with Emily and Charlie, and every night, we sat around the dinner table together. I had so many questions about God, and I took every opportunity to ask them. But my favorite thing was bedtime. Every night of the entire month, my God-given missionary mom would tuck me in bed, read me a psalm from the Bible, and kiss me on the forehead to say goodnight. It was as though God had whispered my secret wish to her. It showed me how personal God was, to meet such a specific need and prayer.

The last night of my stay, Emily invited me to receive Jesus. At the time, I was so worried about "turning" on my Jewish father that I didn't take her up on it. But, as you know from the beginning of this book, I did eventually give my life to Christ, and as a result I lost my Jewish family for ten years (though today they are all born-again Christians). What a mighty God we serve! Emily continued to be a mom for me until she went home to be with the Lord. But I made sure to name my daughter after her so I'd always have a reminder of her love, and I always tell my daughter that.

When I met my husband, God was so sweet because He gave me another mom in my amazing mother-in-law, Janice, whom I affectionately called my "mother-in-love." I was so nervous when I first met her, but then she handed me a beautiful letter that she had written to me when Steve was a baby. I opened the hand-crafted card she created and read: "To My Future Daughter in Love, I've been praying for you since my son was a baby and now I finally get to see your sweet face. We are so glad that you're going to be part of our family!"

I don't think I was exactly what she pictured. I wanted to impress her, so I had on an all-white rhinestone jumpsuit complete with matching rhinestone cowboy boots. You see, I met her on a farm, and back then, I thought all farms were like *Dallas*, the popular soap opera that had overtaken our TVs at the time. I hadn't realized that this was a simple family where nobody so much as touched makeup. There I was, a former beauty queen with false eyelashes and rhinestone armor. I was bringing splatter paints of glitter and color to their black-and-white, simple but wonderful world. But they loved me well—differences and all. They made me feel so at home, so comfortable, and so welcomed in their family.

Honestly, it was like a dream come true! I felt like I was marrying into my dream family. It really was everything I hoped it would be. As you know by now, my marriage was very hard, but the family my husband was born into became the greatest gift God ever gave me. Today my mother-in-law is in Heaven with the Lord; she passed from breast cancer, and not a day goes by that I don't miss her mother's love for me.

Even though I did not have the mom I wanted, God proved His faithfulness by using His family to give me two amazing spiritual moms. They both loved me the way I craved to be loved, and they both brought me closer to God than I ever could have gotten without their love. I believe they were an extension of how much God loves me personally. I also believe their love gave me the grace I would need to forgive my mom. Their examples helped me give my mom the grace she needed from me as a daughter.

The hard part was, I still felt so much pain from the emotional abuse throughout my life that I was constantly being triggered. I bought into the devil's lies that because I had a bad mom, I would also be a bad mom. So when my husband proposed to me, I told him right away that I never wanted to have children because of my experience with my mom. My husband responded perfectly by saying, "Sheri Rose, that's not up to me or you. It's up to God if He gives us a baby or not."

God has a sense of humor and didn't waste any time showing me how powerful He was. I got pregnant on our honeymoon while on two forms of birth control the first time Steve and I were intimate. So much for my plan of not having children! But I wouldn't trade it for the world because it brought us our son Jake, who was a complete joy to raise (which I think was God's redemption for what I went through as a child).

As I was preparing the baby's room, something inside me (I believe it was the Holy Spirit) was screaming that before I gave birth, I needed to go back and do what I could to make things right with my mom. It's not that I didn't want to obey, but I couldn't see a way to get to her heart. As the Holy Spirit began to work with me, I wrestled with every pain from my past regarding my mom. I knew God was merciful and that He'd forgiven me of all my sins as if they'd never happened. But as I wrestled with Him, all I could think was this: *I'm human. I'm not God.*

I felt the Lord reply to me, "But I am in you and I am in your heart. You are in My strength, so you can do anything I ask you to do if you choose to say yes to Me."

I knew my Heavenly Father wanted to free me by telling me something had to shift in the spirit realm through the power of forgiveness. I knew it would not be easy, but I also knew the enemy would do everything he could to stop me and my mom from reconciling. My due date was approaching, and my focus was quickly turning to giving birth and becoming a mom.

I knew the generational curse on my family had to be broken before I gave birth and history repeated itself. I'm sure my mom never wanted to become like hers, but she had never forgiven her mom, and I suffered the consequences of that decision as her child. I did not want my children to suffer the same consequences through my unforgiveness. I desperately needed God's strength to reach out without letting the fear of rejection stop me from doing the right thing.

After a couple months of wrestling with God on this matter, I got up in the middle of the night, walked into my unborn baby boy's room, knelt down by his crib, and began to cry out to my Heavenly Daddy, "God, this is the hardest thing I've ever done, and I need Your help! I need Your strength, and I need You to give me the words to write to my mom."

I stayed in that room, kneeling on the floor and asking God to reveal His presence to me somehow. I honestly could feel Him in the room, and I believe He hurt with me. I felt comfort knowing that He had compassion for me. I got up from the floor and sat on the rocking chair with a pad of paper and a pen. God did give me the words to pour out. Tears flowed down my face onto the paper as I wrote:

Dear Momma,

I know we haven't seen each other for a really long time, but I am no longer a little girl. I am a woman now, and I'm going to become a mom soon. I know our relationship has been hard, but I've always wanted to be close to you, and I believe somehow you want to be close to me too. If there's any way that you received this letter and are reading it, would you consider coming when I give birth to my first baby and holding your first grandchild? By the way, it's a boy. I'm going to have a son!

I love you,

Your Daughter, Sheri Rose

Step one was done. I sealed the letter in an envelope. Now I had to find out where my mom lived. (Back then, we didn't have Google or cell phones; it was over thirty years ago.) Although my dad feared the outcome for me, he knew I really wanted to make this right, so he helped me hire a detective to find my mom's address.

It took me a couple of months to find out where she was living. But every night, I put my hand on that envelope and prayed for my mom's hurting heart. I found that the more I prayed for her, the less I hurt and the more I began to have compassion for her.

A few weeks later, after I was finally able to send the letter, I received a call from our post office saying I had received a package in the mail from a Carole Goodman. This was the call I had been waiting for. I was so excited that she'd not only received and read the letter, but she'd responded by sending a box back.

I was sure it was a baby gift. I was so proud of myself for obeying God and was certain that this was His blessing to me. Once I picked up the box, I sat in the car and stared at it. Before I could open it, I began daydreaming that I was finally going to have the mom that I had always wanted. In my dream, the war was over, and she loved me and my new baby boy like a loving mom would. I wanted friends to come and celebrate with me somehow, so I invited five girlfriends who had always been praying for me and my relationship with my mom over to our house so they could be part of the grand opening of the first box I had ever received from my mom. One of them even brought a cake that said, "Let's celebrate!" I wanted the anticipation to linger as long as it could, so first we cut the cake and each had a bite before one of my friends said it was time to open the box. They all gathered around me on the floor as I opened the gift.

As I lifted the lid off the box, I saw baby clothes inside. But I quickly noticed that all of them were used. Then I thought, *Wow! Maybe she bought these things at a vintage store.* But as I began to pull them out of the box, I realized they were all baby *girl* clothes. I knew I had told her I was having a baby boy. I sat, confused, for a moment and wondered if maybe she had misunderstood. I was so happy to receive a gift from her that I tried to remain in a celebratory state of mind. I took all the girls' clothes out. At the bottom of the box was a birth certificate with a big red arrow pointing to three large handwritten words: "Read the back!"

When I flipped the certificate over, I realized it was my birth certificate and that the clothes in that box had been mine when I was a baby. With trembling hands, I turned my attention to the bottom of the paper, where she had written on my birth certificate "I wish you had never been born, Sheri Rose" in bold red letters. They were followed by: "No one has caused me greater pain than you!"

My girlfriends sat speechless in aching silence, holding me. The pain was more than I could bear. My faith and my heart were destroyed. I know the enemy tried to get me to blame God for her reaction, and to be honest, at first I did. But then I realized that God does not force people's reactions—each person must choose for themselves to love.

I fell with my face to the floor, curled up in a fetal position, and screamed in anguish while my girlfriends gathered around me.

"Why do I have still have to suffer for my mom's sin? It wasn't my fault that they abused her!" I screamed. My friends stood over me with silent tears, unsure what to say. "It wasn't my fault she refused to love me. I was just a little girl...I did not do anything wrong!"

As my sweet friends began to pray over me, silently in my spirit, I heard the Lord whisper, "I didn't do anything wrong either, Sheri Rose, but I went to a cross for you."

As I cried a bucket of tears, I asked my friends to pray that God would show me how to respond so I could release myself from this horrific and painful past before I gave birth to my son. The words of Jesus on the cross came to my mind: "Forgive them, for they know not what they've done."

Even though I knew in my heart that I didn't do anything as a child to hurt my mom, I also knew the only way for me to finally be free was to make the choice to release myself and her by validating her feelings and forgiving her so I could be the mom I wanted to be for my children. I wrestled with God again as I wrote another letter, each word led by His Holy Spirit. I begged Him for a bigger picture than what I was feeling in that moment. I bargained with Him, asking that He would set me free from my past, no matter how she reacted, in exchange for writing this letter.

I knew I could not write it to get my mom to love me. I actually asked her to forgive me for whatever I had done to cause her to regret giving birth to me. Not once in the letter did I bring up what she had done to me.

Those words were written with hopelessness and hurt, and that made it so much harder than the first letter. Those were the hardest, most heart-wrenching words I have ever written on paper, and honestly, nothing in me wanted to send it to her. I didn't think I could emotionally survive another round of my mom's rejection.

But I did not do it for my mom. I wrote it for my God, for my freedom, and for my children's future. The strongest stones laid in our families are the heaviest and the hardest ones for us to lay down. However, as soon as I put that second and final letter in the mail, I felt like the devil was deactivated. I knew I was delivered from my past to a future filled with peace and possibilities!

This story has a bittersweet ending. I never thought I'd hear from my mom again, but I did. She did come to meet her grandchild. It was a strained visit, but at least she was there. Even though it wasn't fun, it was a faith stone laid toward building a new foundation for our relationship. However, even if I had never heard from my mom again, I knew in my heart that love won when I sent that second letter!

When my mom started coming back around, I had to set some very strict boundaries with her to protect myself and my children from getting hurt again. For about five years, I only saw her once a year because that was the safest amount of time to spend with her. But with each visit, she got a little bit softer, and I learned to love her better.

I began to embrace her woman to woman, not daughter to mother. God gave me His heart to let go of everything she hadn't been for me. I realized that she needed a Savior as badly as I did. By our sixth annual visit, I told her about my relationship with Jesus, and she said that she wanted to receive Jesus as her Savior too. I had the privilege of praying with her to receive salvation that day!

Again, it wasn't an overnight change in our relationship, but it was a forever change in her relationship with God. She has grown a lot in the Lord over the years, and I have grown a lot in mercy and grace toward her. These types of circumstances in any family, no matter what the dynamic is, are never easy. But when I stopped being angry about what she wasn't for me, I realized that God was giving my children a live illustration to watch as I loved my mom the most even when she deserved it the least.

WHAT CAN GOD DO?

Today my mom is ninety. She lives with me, and I take care of her. At the moment, we are fighting cancer together. It's still a somewhat difficult relationship. Even though I still have never felt the embrace of her arms around me or heard her express love in a way I wish she would, I realize that one day, when she goes home to be with the Lord, I will live knowing that I loved her well and finished strong in my relationship with her. I will live free of regret because that generational curse was broken by obedient love in action. God has used my mom to teach me how to love the unlovable and how to forgive what I can never forget.

Today I am sixty, and my children are grown. My daughter Emmy is twenty-one and my son Jake is thirty-two. I have three beautiful grandchildren and a godly daughter-in-law, all of whom love and serve God with all their hearts. None of them will ever know the broken woman who raised me because my mom's past sins are where mine are...at the Cross!

WHAT CAN I DO?

Pray and Ask God

When you have been personally hurt by someone you love or someone who should have been there for you, it's hard to think clearly. Start with prayer first and ask God the following questions:

What do You want to do for me?

What do You want to do in me?

What do You want to do through me?

Set Healthy Boundaries

Joseph knew God had a plan for him, and he wasn't about let anyone destroy it, including his brothers. He knew his brothers' deceitful hearts, so he kept a cautious distance and tested their motives and the truth of their words. Just as God was with Joseph through his abuse and imprisonment, He will be with you and will turn what was intended for evil into good. However, this does not mean you should abandon caution and open the door for more abuse. You cannot expect anyone else to value you if you don't value yourself. God values you so much that He sent His Son to die for you. You are valuable! But God doesn't want you to let someone else destroy your body (His temple) with emotional or physical abuse. Forgiveness does not always mean fellowship with the person who hurt you. Sometimes you need to permanently walk away from destructive or abusive relationships.

Pray for Understanding

Truth and understanding always clear the trash out of our thoughts. Leaning into truth gives us a big-picture perspective so we don't have to take everything so personally. Now that I'm a grown woman who has raised two children, I cannot imagine the loneliness and rejection my mom must have experienced when I moved in with my dad. She still had so much unprocessed pain and rejection from her childhood. The rejection of her parents, her abusive first husband, her divorce from my dad, and the pain of her daughter moving out were all piled up and compounding over the years. When I began to understand her heart, it helped me have empathy for her. With that said, while there are reasons for abuse, there are no excuses for it. Abuse, in any form, is always wrong, and you must protect yourself from any further damage from toxic love.

Deal with It or It Will Deal with You

God designed your emotions to serve as warning signs. If you ignore the red light on your dashboard when it tells you it needs gas, eventually, your car is going break down in the middle of nowhere! You are designed the same way. It's imperative you do what you need to in order to get help, whether it's professional counseling or working with a Christian friend to walk through your pain. It will probably require doing hard things like forgiving what you can't forget and releasing yourself from toxic people. You may have to set some strict boundaries, get godly wisdom from the Word, and get godly counseling. Get healing because you deserve to be healed, and you deserve to be free to give and receive love.

Know the Difference between a Bitter Heart and a Broken Heart

A bitter heart wants revenge and will not relent or release the past until it gets it. A bitter heart only feels good when I see those who have hurt me get what they deserve. A broken heart is the result of rejection or toxic love, and that takes time to heal. Don't ever let anybody tell you that you haven't forgiven because you're still hurting. God is close to the brokenhearted, and there will be times when things will trigger that broken heart. When the pain resurfaces, more tears will come, but a touch from the Holy Spirit will heal you again. When you're dealing with abuse, whether it's emotional or physical, you have to use caution and very strict boundaries. If those boundaries are not respected, you need a temporary or complete break from the relationship. In my case, there was total forgiveness, but I knew my mom still had a lot she had to work through personally that I could not help her with. I had to protect my heart and my children's hearts while she was working through her own pain.

His Love Letter to You

My Beloved Daughter,

My heart breaks whenever someone hurts or harms you. I want to reassure you that no unrighteous act is unseen by Me, My love. You never need to give in to the temptation to conquer evil by responding with evil. The enemy of your soul wants you to give in to retaliation. You will lose your integrity any time you attempt to triumph over evil with evil. The only way to protect yourself in the heat of battle is to guard your heart and pray for your enemies so you don't become like them. Revenge only brings pain; My way brings healing to a world filled with heartache and hate. I will deal with the evil that's been done, but I want you to let Me, your Heavenly Father, take care of it for you.

Love,

Your Heavenly Father

"Love is patient and kind. Love is not jealous or boastful or proud or rude. It does not demand its own way. It is not irritable, and it keeps no record of being wronged. It does not rejoice about injustice but rejoices whenever the truth wins out. Love never gives up, never loses faith, is always hopeful, and endures through every circumstance." (1 Corinthians 13:4–7)

Chapter 3

BEYOND SHATTERED

GOD, HELP HEAL MY BROKEN HEART SO I CAN LIVE AND LOVE WITHOUT FEAR AGAIN!

Linda grew up in an amazing Christian family. She had the privilege of being raised by parents who loved each other and her very much. You might say she was sheltered from many things that most of us live in today. As a young girl, she decided that when she grew up, she was going to marry a man just like her dad.

Linda didn't settle for second best. She decided to wait for God's best, and it was worth the wait. She met an amazing man named William, and yes, they had the kind of marriage that women dream of. They had three sons together. She loved being a wife, mom, and homemaker. Honestly, when I think of her, I think about the *Leave It to Beaver* kind of life from the 1950s. She and her hubby had great friends. They lived on a glorious farm filled with orchards, fresh fruits, and vegetables. They had a little dream house with a wraparound porch and worked hard to build a business together. Their hard work paid off, and soon their business flourished. As a result, they were financially blessed.

God gave Linda a wonderful life filled with everything she wanted; she lacked for nothing. In fact, she lived a life that most of us only dream of. (I know it sounds like I'm writing a fantasy story. I can see the birds chirping and Linda breaking out in song right now as I write.) Although she was very blessed, Linda took none of it for granted. She was the kind of person everyone wanted to spend time with because she was so fun, faith-filled, and—to top it all off—a fantastic cook. In all honesty, she is my spiritual mama and one of my most cherished friends. But before you say you can't relate to her story, let me set it up so you can see that rain does fall on every life. No one's life is always sunshine and rainbows. I asked if I could share her very unexpected life-shattering story with you, and she said yes.

It was a crisp Saturday morning in March, and the winter was turning into spring on their quaint Oregon farm. The year was 1984. Linda and her hubby always made time to cuddle in the morning. No, this is not a typo, and yes, after twenty-four years of marriage, they still loved to cuddle. (Maybe that's why they had such a good marriage. I guess it's hard to hold grudges if you're holding each other every day.) When William started to get up to get ready for his day, Linda pulled him back in bed and said, "Hold me a little longer."

The phone rang. It was a business call, so William had to take it. After he got off the phone, he looked at Linda and said, "I'm not feeling well. I think I'd better lie back down." He crawled back in bed with her, and she held him and prayed for her man.

Linda would've loved to stay there forever. Little did she know the day ahead would be the darkest of her life.

Before long, William got up. He was pale. "Honey, you know, I am really not feeling good," he said. He wasn't the kind of man who would complain, so Linda knew it was serious. But nothing could prepare her for what was about to happen to her white-picket-fence family life.

William stretched out on the couch while Linda sat with his head in her lap, praying, "Jesus, please heal my husband."

"Don't worry, honey, I'm sure it's nothing serious. I probably just have a mild flu."

Because they had both been blessed with good health throughout their marriage, she decided to let him rest. Linda went to the kitchen to heat up some homemade chicken soup—the secret cure that always made her husband feel better. She wanted desperately to believe that everything was OK, so she walked out to their back porch and set the table for them where they could look out at the beautiful view of their farm.

"I have something that will make you feel so much better," she told William. "I made your favorite soup out on the porch!"

He smiled at her and said, "Honey, I love you so much. You always know how to make me feel better."

She smiled and exhaled a sigh of relief. But when William stood up to join her, he grabbed his chest and cried, "Something hurts!" Then he fell back down on the couch.

She dropped the bowl of soup she was holding on the carpet and rushed to his side. Her heart sank; deep down in her soul she knew her greatest fear of losing the man she loved might soon become her reality. She prayed so hard, "Please Lord, please Lord, don't let this be real!"

Her youngest son, fourteen-year-old Ron, heard her scream and ran into the room. He saw mom holding his unconscious dad. "How can I help him?" he asked, bewildered.

"Ron, call 911! Call 911 right now!"

Linda's whole life flashed before her while they waited for the ambulance to arrive. What would she ever do without this man she loved so much? Thoughts about the life they had built together ran through her mind. In a blur of panic, she wondered what would happen to their beautiful life if William was gone. Their 2,500-acre farm, the successful manufacturing business they had started just a couple years ago, their picture-perfect house they had designed and built together, their three sons who were almost all adults now…Ron was about to enter high school, and the others were out of the house. Linda was looking forward to many more years with her husband.

While she was playing out all those scenarios in her mind, Linda looked up to see Ron looking at his dad, his sweet face riddled with terror. Linda's heart filled with fear. She was overwhelmed, knowing that she could not comfort Ron because she was so scared herself. She feared Ron would soon have to step up to be the man of the house. His dad was his best friend. How could he lose him?

Linda cried out in prayer, "God, please help us!"

Minutes later, the ambulance arrived, but it was too late. One of the EMTs had been specially trained in cardiac emergencies, and he said it appeared an aneurysm had burst in a major blood vessel near William's heart.

"I am so sorry," he told Linda. "There's nothing we can do for him. He's gone."

She already knew; she had felt his spirit leave the moment it happened. She held him for hours afterward anyway. She was devastated and couldn't handle the thought of her new reality. The living room that once felt so warm and homey now felt dark and pitiful. It held so many memories of their little boys growing up, playing games, and reading together. Many dreams were talked about in this room. Friends and their children had spent many happy hours here. The room that had always been filled with her best memories now also held her worst nightmare.

As she lay on the couch holding her beloved husband's breathless body, Linda felt like she couldn't breathe. With one last desperate cry she screamed, "How could this be happening? He is only forty-three years old! God, I'm not created to do life alone! How am I supposed to live without this man? You raised Lazarus from death to life. Please, God, give me back my husband!" In that moment, no one and nothing could comfort her. Every piece of her heart and home had been utterly shattered. Linda felt herself drowning in despair. She felt so hopeless, helpless, and alone for the first time.

She thought about their older sons. They weren't there, and they didn't get to say goodbye or hug William one last time. She worried about how hard not being able to say goodbye to their dad would be for them. But then again, neither she nor Ron had really had the chance to say goodbye either.

"Oh," she thought, "if only we could have said goodbye." A new round of sobs poured out of her. She thought she'd already cried all she could cry in one day, but she was wrong. The tears began to flow again.

Their middle son, Lance, who was turning twenty the next day, had been planning a father-son birthday trip with William.

Their oldest son, Matt, had just gotten married, and now his father wouldn't be there to give him marriage advice or to see his future grandchildren. So many dreams died with William that day. Linda felt dead on the inside. From that day forward, everything she had known would be different.

Lance and Matt arrived. They knelt beside her and cried with her. None of them ever wanted to let go. While they were holding each other and their father, there was a knock at the door. It was the mortuary van, which had come to pick up William's body. Linda was paralyzed by agony.

The following days were a blur—so much to do, so many decisions to make. She tried to be strong for her sons, but they ended up being stronger for her. She'd always been the one to comfort people in pain, but she never really related to what true heartbreak felt like until now. She knew the Scriptures, she went to church, she was a good Christian woman, but now her faith was put to the test by tears, trials, and a terrifying fear of her future.

She had many friends and family members who were there for her, but nothing really seemed to help the awful pain that burned in her broken heart. She was so lonely. She longed to see William's pick-up truck drive up for lunch again, but it never did. She dreamt about seeing his beautiful smile, but it wasn't there. "How can I ever go on without hearing his wonderful voice singing about our Jesus, whom he loved so much?"

Getting in bed at night was the most painful thing because there were no arms there to hold her. She would lie there in tears, asking the Holy Spirit to comfort her. There were many nights when she could feel God's comfort as she cried until morning. Yes, she had the comforting hope of Heaven, and knowing she and William would meet again, but she longed to have her husband back.

Many well-meaning Christians would say, "Oh, honey, now you just need to let go of William and let Jesus be your husband." She knew they meant well, but it wasn't a comfort at all. It made her feel worse. She loved Jesus with all her heart, but she wanted the husband she loved too.

One of her close friends even said, "Oh, Linda, do you ever want to just give up on God because you had such a wonderful life and He took it all away from you, and now you're just heartbroken and sad every day? It's hard for me to believe that you would still want to serve Him."

That did it! Righteous anger rose up inside Linda as she responded, "Why would I curse the only promise I have of ever seeing William again? God is the only One who has the power to get me through this pain!"

Linda realized it was time to learn to trust God all over again. She thought she had always trusted Him, but that was when she had a husband to provide for her and give her love. Now that she was on her own again, it made her wonder about God. Did He really know her needs? Could she trust Him to do the best thing for her life? Her mind said yes, but her broken heart was battling to believe that it could ever be healed, let alone love again. She knew that God had the power to heal her broken heart, but it wasn't happening fast enough to bring relief from the deep grief that coated her from the inside out.

She did her best to survive in her new reality, but everywhere she looked, all she could see were the memories of her marriage. It hurt so badly that she decided she needed to go somewhere to try to escape the emotional torment she felt every day. She knew she needed to revive her love relationship with the Lord in order to get through the gravity of the grief that was pulling her down.

The next day, a good friend invited her to go on a tour of Israel. *There's no better place than the Holy Land to feel close to God*, Linda thought. She dragged herself off the couch and booked the tour.

When she got off the plane in Israel, Linda prayed quietly, "God, please meet me here." She wanted a personal encounter with the Lord so desperately. God answered her prayer on the last stop of the tour. There she was in the Garden of Gethsemane. Could there be a better place to meet with God than right where Jesus experienced His greatest grief before going to the cross?

While Linda roamed, she reflected on Jesus's desperate cry to His father for another way. She would have given anything to have another way—why did she have to face the death of her husband? Something in her became so desperate for healing that she fell to the ground and prayed, "Heavenly Father, please heal my heart so I can love again." She continued by praying these words of Jesus: "But not my will, Lord...I want Your will to be done for the rest of my life. Amen." She stayed on her face for a while and wept.

All of a sudden, she could feel the presence of the Holy Spirit comforting her in a way she'd never felt before. She had always known God's comfort, but in an instant, she felt a calming to her soul and a nourishing of her spirit. In that moment of surrender to God's will, the Holy Spirit gave her an overwhelming peace, knowing that God had heard her heart's cry. She knew that in His perfect timing, He would give her the desire of her heart.

When she got back from her trip, Linda decided to start dating a few Christian men who had pursued her previously. But nothing felt right with any of them. She continued to hold on to the hope that she had felt in the Garden of Gethsemane. As God continued to take her through the grieving process, she started to notice some good days come in between the bad. She began to breathe again. She could feel that healing truly was happening in her heart, and she knew that God was somehow taking the pieces of it to make something beautiful out of her brokenness—like a stained-glass window!

As she began to fall more and more in love with her Jesus, she knew He was preparing her heart to love again. Even though she could not physically see a man she could marry, she knew in her heart that she could trust her Heavenly Father in His perfect time to bring the man He picked for her.

Linda began to enjoy the flowers on her farm again, and watching the food grow brought her a renewed joy as she saw the hopefulness in the land's entering a new season. She even started cooking again and having family over to enjoy her meals. She knew she was going into a new season, and she had to get ready for it. Linda didn't want the new season to be her rescue; she wanted God to rescue her so she could step into her new season on solid faith. After her husband's death, she saw how dangerous it was to put her faith in her family, so she sought to keep God first for the rest of her life.

All three of her sons could see she was ready to step into a new season, and they knew they needed to give her the courage to do so. They found an amazing ministry in Hawaii called Youth with a Mission, which offered three-month mission trip opportunities, and thought, *Well, there's a romantic place for her to meet a Christian man—plus, she loves the ocean.*

The boys wanted to help their mom get back out there. They felt she would fit perfectly in YWAM's ministry. She was great at raising kids, but they were grown. They knew she needed a way to use her gifts for God. Of course, as they knew she would, she made all kinds of excuses for why she couldn't leave them or her business. But they assured her they would take care of everything and that they would all be perfectly fine if she left for a bit. They *made* her go. (I think they were so desperate to get their mom on a new mission that they would've gotten her into a rowboat and rowed her across the ocean to put her on that island.)

Knowing Linda, I think deep down she was thankful, but the unknown can be intimidating. But she knew God was with her and she trusted Him to get her where He wanted her next. So she took another leap of faith, booked the trip, and off she went.

On her flight to Kona, Linda felt God reassuring her of the promise He had given her in the Garden of Gethsemane; He was going to give her a new beginning. For the first time in years, she didn't cry tears of sadness, but instead cried tears of hope.

While in Hawaii, Linda was sharing her story with a woman she had met; it turned out the woman worked in publishing, and she asked Linda if she would be willing to write a book about her life. Linda was a little surprised, but as she considered it, she worried that writing about her life might resurrect all the pain she had worked so hard to get through. On the other hand, maybe it would help others through their grief as well. So she said yes.

To her surprise, writing out all the details actually gave Linda a chance to work through every little thing. This writing exercise was exactly what she needed to mourn and heal more before the next chapter of her life began. (And yes, the book is very good, and it does help many people get through the gates of grief with the help of God.)

When Linda returned from Hawaii, her best friends surprised her with a weekend writing class in Salem, Oregon. On the first day, she recognized the teacher, but couldn't recall where she had seen him before. Then she remembered that she and William had heard the man speak at a Christian convention in Hawaii years before. His name was Don, and he had spoken about the tragedy of losing his wife. She remembered how sorry she had felt for him when she heard him speak. She had no idea at the time that she would be a widow one day as well.

As Linda stared at Don that first day, trying to remember why he seemed familiar, he thought she was checking him out—and he liked it.

Don is the kind of man who goes for what he wants. So when Linda stepped outside after class, he bolted after her. He quickly navigated through the crowd in the hallway and out the door to find her. Surprisingly, she was nowhere to be seen. He asked some friends, "Do you know who that pretty lady was who popped into my class while I was teaching?"

They smiled and told him, "Oh, she's our friend. She is a widow who lives near Eugene. We invited her to come up and be part of your writing class this week."

Little did Linda or Don know that their mutual friends had all of this in mind when they invited both of them to take part in the class, hoping they might "click." I guess you could say it was a secret set-up with the Lord's leading.

Don's friends could tell he was smitten by Linda, and they encouraged him to ask her out to lunch. He really didn't need encouragement; he was going to ask her anyway.

The next day, he made sure he was everywhere she was. It actually made her feel a little uncomfortable, but he knew he needed to wait for the right opportunity to ask her out. When he overheard her sharing her story of being widowed, he chimed in and shared some details about his own experience. He asked if she wanted to go to lunch after class, and she said yes.

That afternoon, Linda sat across the table from Don and watched him as he spoke. *Wow, he doesn't even look like the same guy I saw in Kona. He doesn't look nearly as old as he did then. I guess grief really can take a toll when you're in it. Actually, I think he is really cute,* she thought as she smiled at him from across the table. She got a little giddy. *Am I actually attracted to another man?* Then she said a quick silent prayer: *God, is this You or just a good-looking guy across the table with all the right words?*

Linda was a smart girl. She let Don be the man and pursue her, and that's exactly what he did. He pursued her week after week while she struggled with many mixed emotions. He was nothing like William, and she was nothing like his wife, Betty. Looking back, she realized what a good thing that was because it didn't trigger memories of anything familiar for either of them. Each of them was in new territory with each other, and that turned out to be a blessing.

Linda and Don spent many days and endless hours together. The more she learned about him, the more interested she became. She was falling in love again. She longed to be married again, and everything seemed so right. Most of all, Don loved God more than anything, and that was so important to her. Don lived close by her sons and her business. Maintaining a relationship was easy and convenient. If they ended up together, she wouldn't have to move far away to be with him. Don was a successful businessman whom she wouldn't have to support. Because he had lost his wife, he understood her heart when she said, "I will always love William." He assured her that he would always love Betty too. In fact, he said at one point in his grieving process, he wasn't sure if he ever wanted to remarry because he wanted to spend eternity with Betty.

Wow! He loved Betty the same way that I loved William. That's amazing! Linda thought.

Everything was happening so fast; it felt wonderful to have a godly man beside her. It didn't hurt that she was also very attracted to him, and she loved the way he doted on her and gave her his full attention. She said it seemed like he would ask her a hundred questions every time they were together. She loved that he was so interested in who she was and what she had to say.

But Linda wanted to be completely sure that God had given her this new love, so she decided to test her own heart one last time. She scheduled a four-week mission trip to get away, reflect, and pray. She knew if she laid this love down at God's feet, He would show her if Don was indeed the one she was supposed to marry.

There were so many questions on her mind during that time. Would his family accept her? Would her boys accept him? Could she really love someone else enough to marry again?

She had just finished writing the book about her life, but it hadn't been published yet. Linda was having dinner with Don a few days before her trip when he asked her if he could have a copy of her manuscript to read while she was gone. He said he wanted to get to know her even better. She agreed to share her manuscript, and then in a cute, flirty way, she asked him, "What can I read of yours to get to know *you* better?"

"Hmmm, let's see…you wouldn't like to read my doctoral dissertation—it's boring!" he replied with a chuckle. "I know—I've got some journals that I have been writing the past five years. Would you want to look at those?"

Linda studied his face to see if he was joking, but he seemed serious. "Really? Are you sure? Journals are pretty personal."

"I'd love to share them with you. I think they might help you see my true heart before I met you," he responded confidently.

A few days later, Don took Linda to the airport. When he got out of the car to hug her goodbye, he handed her his personal journals, and she gave him her unpublished manuscript. They prayed together before they said goodbye.

Linda couldn't wait to start reading Don's journals. Luckily for her, it was a long flight to the Philippines for her mission trip, so she snuggled up with them on the plane. With each page, she cried and realized that she loved Don more than she ever thought possible. Her heart broke open to his love when she saw his heart poured out in such a personal way.

But what she wasn't expecting were the pages he had journaled during their whirlwind courtship. On the very last page, he described in detail what God had shown him about her throughout their courtship.

And he used his final journal entry to ask her to marry him.

Instantly, Linda started crying. The flight attendant came over to see if she was OK, and through sobs, Linda replied, "A man I love just proposed to me, and I am going to say yes!" The flight attendant looked at her like she was a little crazy—there was no man around Linda on the plane.

So she asked, "Where is the man who proposed to you? We'd love to congratulate you in front of everybody on this flight!"

"Oh my," Linda chuckled through her joyful tears. "He's not on this plane; he's back in the United States. He asked me in his journal. He wrote that he wants to marry me, and I am saying *yes*!" Then she began to share her story of grief with the flight attendant—everything that had brought her to that moment. The more she talked, the more other passengers began to listen. Soon, there was a small crowd gathering around to hear her story. Many people were getting ministered to by her testimony of how faithful and powerful God is. For the first time, she was able to see how her grief could get people to see God.

She recalled the Garden of Gethsemane, where she had cried out to God and related to Jesus's grief in asking for another way. At the time, she could see no way out of the heart-wrenching ache of missing William every day. But sitting there on the plane, she could see in that moment how God really does work all things together for good for those who are in Christ Jesus, even after a tragedy. She was grateful that she hadn't given up her faith when life got hard or heartbreaking.

When the plane landed, she ran to a phone booth and made a collect call to Don (back then, they didn't have cell phones). When he answered, she enthusiastically yelled, "Yes!" and they both cried tears of celebration over the phone. They didn't let the fifty-dollars-a-minute collect phone call from the Philippines impede their joy. While they were racking up charges, Don announced that he didn't want to wait any longer: he wanted to buy Linda a first-class ticket to fly directly to Hawaii so they could get married as soon as she returned from her mission trip.

It was a little overwhelming trying to figure out how to plan a wedding and get all their family members to Hawaii with only four weeks' notice. But Don is a man who knows how to make things happen, so he convinced her. "Trust me. Just say yes, and I'll make it happen!"

She said if he could get all their children to Kona at that time, she would consent to this crazy timetable. "I love you so much that I know I want to spend the rest of my life with you! I just didn't expect it to be the day I got off the plane from my mission trip. But if you can make it happen, then I'll be there." She found herself a dress in the Philippines and even wore her veil on the plane trip to Hawaii so that she could tell everybody along the way that she was on the way to her wedding.

The day her mission trip ended and she boarded that flight, she couldn't believe she was off to meet her husband and to be with her entire family. When she stepped off the plane, everybody was there to meet her. The friends who had set them up had helped Don pick out the flowers and coordinate the wedding. Linda and the group that met her at the airport were picked up by a limo, and they set out together for a gorgeous resort on the beach.

It was a perfect evening for a wedding—seventy degrees without too much wind and no clouds. Linda said it was the most glorious, redeeming God moment of her life.

Don and Linda honeymooned in Kona. They loved it so much that they later bought a house there.

They've now been married thirty-four years. Yes, they both still have days when they grieve for their first loves. But they give each other the freedom to keep those memories alive. They will forever be grateful that God put them together to spend the rest of their days loving Him and loving each other. Today, they are in full-time ministry together, and they've had many God adventures. They're both extroverts and love to talk, so they've had to learn how to take turns listening. Between them they have six children, fifteen grandchildren, and nine great-grandchildren. That's a lot of different personalities in one big combined family, but they've learned how to navigate them all well. They even wrote a book together about second marriages called *To Love Again*.

In perfect fairytale fashion, the book was released on their tenth anniversary.

WHAT CAN GOD DO?

God Can Use Death to Save a Life

I want share one short story so you can see the different ways God can use the dismantling of our lives.

A young couple rushed their unconscious three-year-old daughter, Rose, to the hospital. They held each other and cried as the doctors said they would give their daughter one more round of medicine—the eleventh attempt to get her heart working. The couple got on their knees and prayed a desperate prayer for their daughter's heart to start beating. Within moments, Rose's heart began to beat again.

Rose was put on life support for the next ten days. She never showed any sign of brain activity, and as hard as it was, her parents knew early on that their little girl was in the arms of Jesus. They could see she was suffering, so they selflessly prayed for her to "go home" because they didn't want her to suffer any longer. It was painful to see her perfect-looking body lying there in bed, knowing she wasn't ever going to wake up.

Of course, in their humanity, they wondered why God answered their prayer for her heart to beat again but didn't heal her brain.

They spent the next few days holding their sweet daughter, trying to prepare emotionally for something no parent ever wants to prepare for: to let her go home to be with Lord. When the doctors presented them with an opportunity for Rose to become an organ donor, they immediately felt led by the Lord to do so. In that moment, they realized the reason Rose's heart had started beating again was not only for them to have a little more time with her; it was also to give someone else's child a new chance at life.

Somehow, it made their final goodbye with Rose more peaceful, knowing that her heart would still be beating here on Earth in someone else's chest, and they prayed for whoever that person would be.

The next day, they learned through an internet broadcast about sweet Daniel, a one-year-old who had been in a Canadian hospital for ninety days awaiting a heart transplant. They wondered if he could be the recipient they had prayed for. Rose's parents felt a supernatural, overwhelming joy when they realized Daniel's family also had been praying for a miracle—and he did receive Rose's heart.

In the years that followed, God gave Rose's parents three more daughters. He also made a way for Rose's mom to meet Daniel's mom. They each shared their stories of what God can do even in the midst of tragedy, and to this day, they are still friends.

WHAT CAN I DO?

Give Yourself Grace to Grieve

If you have suffered the loss of a loved one, a parent, a child, a spouse, or a best friend, that kind of grief has a gravity that's impossible to withstand. You must take time to grieve—there's just no way around it. In the Psalms, David cried a lot. Your Heavenly Father says what you sow with tears you will reap with joy. Solomon, the wisest man who ever lived, says there is a season for sorrow, and that season needs to be complete in order to move on to the next season. When you're in a serious, brokenhearted, internal battle, you've got to give yourself grace to process. Just remember, the pain-filled version of yourself isn't who you are. You are in a season of suffering that will eventually come to an end. But in this season, you have to let go of anything you don't have to do and anything or anyone who puts demands on you so you can get fully healed. The Word of God says the truth will set us free, and those who sow with tears will reap with joy.

Reach Out

If you know a grieving person don't let fears about saying or doing the wrong thing stop you from reaching out. Just ask someone who has lost a loved one. Let your grieving loved one know you're there to listen, love, and help any way you can. Be sure to listen and not ask too many questions. Find practical ways to help (laundry, cooking, errands). Continue your support after the funeral or tragedy.

Get Real with God

Grief may involve extreme emotions and behaviors. Feelings of guilt, anger, despair, and fear are common. When you're grieving, you might yell at God or cry for hours on end. Let me reassure you that what you feel is normal. Don't judge yourself or others if you're helping someone through grief. No one is quite themselves when they are in the midst of grieving. I always compare it to how, when a lifeguard is saving someone, he acts very differently than a person who is drowning and needs to be saved.

His Love Letter to You

My Beloved Daughter,

I never expect you to handle the heartache of this life by yourself. Tears are a gift from Me. I want you to cry out to Me whenever you're hurting, knowing that I hear your heart and I catch every tear. The things you see that break your heart break My heart also, so be careful not to allow the enemy to convince you it's Me causing the pain. I sent My Son to bind up the wounds of the brokenhearted, but the enemy of your soul comes to break your heart. That's why I tell you to guard your heart. I want you to be careful who you give your heart to and who you share your heart with. Let Me be your safe place when you cry. Give Me a chance to heal your broken heart. I promise if you come to Me, you will feel My presence and experience My miraculous peace and joy that always comes in the morning after a good cry to your Heavenly

Daddy. I am here, wanting and willing to walk you out of this grief and into a great new beginning.

Love,

Your Heavenly Father

"He heals the brokenhearted and bandages their wounds." (Psalm 147:3)

Chapter 4

Beyond Shame

God, give me the grace to forgive myself for what I have done and believe I am a new creation.

My dad had a way with words. He could always present things in a way that inspired me to do the right thing. He often did this by giving me a glimpse of what the outcome in a particular situation might be. He wasn't a Christian man when he was raising me, but he was a wise man, and he knew how to inspire and instruct very well.

When I turned sixteen, he took me out to dinner and said he wanted to have a talk with me about boys and sex. Because he was the one who raised me, I guess he was left doing that for his daughter. He told me that if I wanted to feel like a treasure and have boys treat me well, I should not have sex with them. Well, there you have it. His talk was short, sweet, and to the point.

He was right. Although the boys did treat me differently (in a good way, because they couldn't have their way with me), I still felt curious, and I was left out of many of my girlfriends' conversations about their sexual adventures with their boyfriends. I honestly felt like I was the only virgin left out of all the fun. "*Fun*" has always been one of my top priorities, so the thought of missing out on anything made it even more difficult to remain pure.

Looking back now, I can see that Satan planted that seed in me as a set-up to tempt me to surrender to sex. One night when my friends, my boyfriend, and I were all smoking pot, partying, and pigging out, they dared me to crawl in the back of my boyfriend's van and have sex with him. In a moment of weakness, my curiosity conquered me, and I caved. Talk about a "cheap date" and being "young and dumb"!

Too much pot, some Taco Bell, and he had me in the back of his van.

The next day at school, rumors spread quickly. Everybody was asking me to spill the dirty details. To be honest, I liked the attention. But because I was so stoned when it happened, I didn't remember any of the details. I decided to just make them up, as I'm sure all my friends had as well. Since I'd been left out of so many conversations, I wanted to outdo everybody else's sexual adventure stories.

Six weeks later, I started feeling extremely nauseous. Every day after lunch, I was running to the bathroom and throwing up at school. I was a teenager, and I did not track my period, so it never occurred to me that I had missed one or that I could be pregnant. Plus, my boyfriend had used a condom that night, so I thought I was safe. One day, the nausea got so out of control that the school nurse called my dad to take me to the emergency room. The nausea was horrible, but nothing compared to the embarrassment and shame I felt after the doctor ran blood tests.

I'll never forget when he came into the room with his clipboard and white coat on. He asked me, "Have you been sexually active in the last six weeks?"

Because I didn't want my dad to be disappointed, I lied to the doctor. I looked at him and replied, "Of course not! The answer is absolutely no!"

"Well, that's interesting—because you're pregnant," he said matter-of-factly.

The heartbreak I saw on my dad's face and the shame I felt in that moment will never leave me. The doctor sat with me and my dad and asked, "Well, what would you like to do?"

My first thought was, *I'd like to go back to my purity and undo that dreadful night.* I didn't even remember the night, and it was certainly not worth the position it put me in: terrified and regretful in that doctor's office. I had a knot and a baby in my belly, and I certainly was not prepared to become a mom at sixteen years of age. All I could see was how that one bit of curiosity caused everything to change for the rest of my life. I began to cry uncontrollably in front of my dad and the doctor.

My dad came over to me and held me. He looked me in the eye and comforted me. "We will get through this, baby girl."

As we sat there, the doctor chimed in, "You know, you don't have to have this baby."

"What do you mean?" I asked, confused at first. "Oh, you mean I could put it up for adoption?"

"No," said the doctor. "We can do a procedure called an abortion, and it will be like this never happened."

"What do you mean?" I don't think I quite understood. Looking back, knowing what I know now, I cannot believe how casual he was about taking a baby out of my belly.

As my dad and I drove back home, I couldn't even talk. To make matters worse, I was still severely nauseous, and now the nausea came from more than just the pregnancy. I was confused and oh so scared.

When we got home, my stepmom greeted us at the door. My dad gave her a serious look and suggested we all sit down to have a talk. I told them I would do whatever they told me to do. By the end of the conversation, the decision was made for me. My stepmom scheduled an appointment for an abortion and told me she would go with me. None of us were Christians at the time, and none of us really understood the ramifications I would later experience from that choice.

The next morning, my stepmom took me to get "the procedure," as they called it. I'll never forget driving to the clinic. I had this sick feeling in my spirit, but I didn't know why. I am very rarely silent, but in that moment, I literally had nothing to say. I vividly remember fighting an internal battle as I walked into the clinic. Upon check-in, the nurse saw fear on my face and reassured me I was doing the right thing by choosing to end the pregnancy. Something about that word, "choosing," immediately chained me to guilt. I kept thinking that if I had just taken my father's advice, I wouldn't be in this place.

I looked around the waiting room. There were ten other teenage girls waiting to terminate their pregnancies. I couldn't help but wonder about each of their stories. We all sat in sad silence as the nurse walked to each one of us, handed us a pill and a gown, and told us to change. She explained that the pill would relax us so we wouldn't feel anything.

When the nurse got to me, I looked in her eyes and said, "May I ask you a question? I am eight weeks pregnant. Does the baby in my belly have a heartbeat?"

"Oh no, absolutely not! There is no heartbeat until twelve weeks. Right now, it is just a formation of cells that we are cleaning out of your uterus." She looked at me, seeing that I still wasn't sure about the situation, and continued, "Don't worry, sweetie, you're doing the responsible, right thing."

With that, I took the pill she gave me. Within twenty minutes, I began to feel very out of it. But I could still hear a voice in my head telling me, *This is not right.* Just when I wanted to run out of the room, the nurse returned and said, "It's your turn, sweetie. Get in the wheelchair, and we'll roll you into the procedure room so the doctor can take care of you."

As two nurses were helping me out of the wheelchair and up onto the table, my heart hurt. I could not figure out the conflict inside myself. After all, I was a teenager. I wasn't ready to be a mom.

It was "the best thing for the baby." But if that were true, then why did I feel so sick inside?

I sat up on the table with tears welling up, looked right into the doctor's eyes, and said, "Promise me this baby doesn't have a heartbeat yet."

"We've already told you several times. A baby doesn't have a heartbeat until it is twelve weeks old. You were only eight weeks. We're just removing particles before the heart starts beating."

We didn't have Google or cell phones back then. There was a lot less access to information, especially as young as I was. We trusted doctors to tell us the truth, especially as teenagers. I was shaking physically and couldn't stop crying. Everyone in the room could tell I was about to freak out, so without my permission, the nurse gave me a shot that knocked me out completely.

All I remember after that was waking up in a lot of pain. I felt like I was a wreck physically and emotionally as they wheeled me back to the waiting room. My dad and stepmom were both there waiting for me, but I couldn't look at either of them. They kept me there for a while because I was bleeding so badly. Once the bleeding slowed down, they helped me to the car and drove me home.

The whole way home, I cried. But the full reality of what had happened didn't hit me until twelve years later. By that time, I was twenty-eight years old and pregnant with my firstborn, Jake. (I actually got pregnant while on my honeymoon and on birth control. So there you go—the first time I had sex with my boyfriend, I got pregnant, and then the first time I had sex with my husband, I got pregnant. I guess it's safe to say I'm a "Fertile Myrtle.")

Right away, I was extremely nauseous again. My husband, Steve, took me to the doctor to confirm how far along I was in my pregnancy. I remember walking into the room and hearing the doctor say, "Today we are going to perform an ultrasound so we can see and hear your baby's heartbeat."

I was completely confused. "Doctor, what do you mean? I know I can't be more than eight weeks pregnant. It doesn't have a heartbeat yet, right?"

The doctor giggled at how little I knew and said, "Well, let's find out!" Then he put the little ultrasound wand on my belly, and I heard my son's heartbeat. "You're right, it looks like you are exactly eight weeks pregnant."

The moment I heard the sound of my son's heartbeat, I burst into tears. I had never told my husband about the abortion. At the time, he thought I was crying tears of joy. Only I knew that I was crying tears of terror as I realized I had been lied to. I was so angry, ashamed, and awakened to what I had done. I was so worried now. On top of the shame, I became terrified that I needed to tell my husband about what I had done. Because I was led to believe an abortion was no big deal, I had never thought it mattered if he knew about it or not.

There's an old saying: "Knowledge is power," but in my case, this knowledge was torment. I became overwhelmed by the whole thing. What should've been the most exciting moment in my life—giving birth to my first baby—instead turned into a personal hell. Instead of joy, all I could feel was morning sickness, shame, sadness, and unexplained fears that my baby would die in birth as punishment for what I had done as a teenager.

When I was nine months pregnant, we left California to live in Arizona near my mother-in-law, who was my best friend. I didn't have a relationship with my mom, so she was the only mom I felt loved by. (You know you love someone when you leave sunny California's seventy-degree days while nine months pregnant to move to one-hundred-and-twenty-degree Arizona in August!)

For the first two years of my son's life, I felt sure that he would be killed as a consequence of my choice as a young girl to abort a baby. I was sure that my five months of nausea and being hooked up to IVs to keep me hydrated was punishment from God. The secret shame stayed with me for years, and so did the fear of my child dying. Once I gave birth safely, I adored Jake—he was a very fun son. But the joy of motherhood was being stolen from me by my sobering secret and shame.

As time passed, God began to open up doors for me as a Christian speaker. I felt unworthy to be in ministry because the secret kept me bound up to shame, and I didn't know how to break free.

When I was thirty-nine my husband had a vasectomy. The night before his surgery, I got pregnant with our daughter. I'd always wanted a little girl but never thought my dream would come true. You see, I'd had three miscarriages after giving birth to Jake. Once again, I convinced myself that my miscarriages were punishment for the abortion. Back then, I definitely didn't understand the mercy and grace of my loving Heavenly Father.

The day after Steve's vasectomy, I remember going to a girlfriend's birthday party. One of the women there had just had a baby girl and asked if I would mind holding her baby girl while she used the restroom. When she put that baby girl in my arms, I began to cry at the thought of never having another child. I was overcome by the grief that I would never have the daughter I had dreamt about. Little did I know that I was already pregnant. I silently cried out to God. I felt like I didn't deserve to have the desire of my heart after what I had done. I now realize that was Satan's voice and nothing remotely like the voice of my God.

Three weeks later, I was speaking at a Christian book show. I still didn't know I was pregnant. I shared how I had always wanted a daughter, but it was now too late because my husband had been fixed and so had our dog. All the women laughed. While I was signing books later, a woman approached me and said, "While you were speaking today, God showed me that you're pregnant with the little girl you always wanted." Honestly, I thought she was crazy, and I didn't pay much attention.

That night, I heard an aggressive knock on my hotel door. When I answered, that same lady was standing there holding two pregnancy tests. "Hi, Sheri Rose, it's me again. I could tell earlier that you didn't really believe what I had to say to you. So I have an easy solution! I brought you these pregnancy tests. You go in the bathroom and pee on both of these sticks, and I will wait right here so you know that what I told you is true."

I guess she knew it would take two sticks for me to believe. I went ahead and humored the woman by taking the tests. To my shock, a few minutes later, I was sitting in that bathroom staring at a positive test result. It was true—I was pregnant with the little girl I desired!

Again, I experienced five months of severe nausea and still believed this was my second round of punishment for abortion. When I was nine months pregnant with my daughter, I had my last speaking engagement before I gave birth. My flight home was immediately after the event, so the second it ended, we had to rush to the airport. I hurried to our car, but before we could pull away, a teenage girl ran up and banged on the window to get my attention. As I rolled the window down, she handed me a piece of paper and told me to take it into the birthing room when it was time to deliver my baby.

On the paper was a verse that read, "Your baby will live and not die, says the Lord."

Now that's just what every pregnant woman wants to hear right before she goes into delivery! You can imagine the fear that crept up on me as my due date came and went. Emmy ended up being two weeks late. I was so ready to push that baby out that I would literally ask people if they had any furniture I could move to push me into labor. When it finally came time to have the baby, something made me grab that piece of paper before leaving the house on our way to the hospital. I'm not going to lie—I was very afraid that this would be the baby who would die during birth. I still felt undeserving of such a gift.

My greatest fear became reality when my sweet Emmy came out totally gray and not breathing. Her umbilical cord was wrapped around her neck three times and strangling her with every push during labor. The nurses and doctors put her on a table in the corner and started pumping her lungs to see if they could get her to breathe. Seven minutes passed, but to me it felt like an eternity.

The doctors continued to work furiously, pumping air into her lungs. While they did, I literally screamed out the verse God promised, "My baby will live and not die!" In the eighth minute, Emmy gasped and then let out a scream. Tears streamed down my face as I heard my daughter take her first breath. She was rushed to the NICU immediately. Because I was older and the birth had been so traumatic, once she took a breath, I went into shock for about an hour on the table. I couldn't feel anything, and I couldn't respond to anyone around me. I could see my best friend, Rochelle, and I could see my husband and the doctor who delivered our baby, but I felt completely numb. They eventually got me into a room. Two days went by, and I still hadn't been able to see my baby face-to-face.

The hospital brought in a brain specialist from Portland. I remember him coming into the room and telling me my baby would be brain-dead and that it would be best to let her go. But this time, I was not going to give up, and I was not going to let go. I'd already had one doctor talk me into letting go of a baby when I was sixteen. I wasn't going to let that happen again. My fear turned into faith, and I began to believe that God could do a miracle. The following night, which happened to be the third, a nurse came into my room to take my vitals. She looked at my wristband, saw my name, and asked if I was Sheri Rose Shepherd, the author.

I was groggy but replied, "I am...of the book *His Princess*."

She began to cry, telling me how the book had helped her through a crisis. Then she said, "I am so sorry—I just saw your baby in the NICU."

I told her the doctor had told me my baby girl would be brain-damaged and deaf if she survived. "Well, there's one way to know for certain," she said. "Should we go find out?"

"How in the world would I be able to do that?" I asked desperately.

"Let me go get the other nurse, and we will wheel you up to see your girl."

It was the first time I had gotten to see my baby face-to-face in three days. She was hooked up to countless tubes and IVs, isolated in her tiny incubator.

The NICU nurse gently asked, "Do you want to try to nurse her? Then we can know for sure if she has suffered brain damage."

"How would that show if she has brain damage or not?" I asked.

The nurse explained that a baby with brain damage usually cannot latch on and nurse. Through all the tubes, they lifted Emmy up and placed her on my breast. I was amazed: Not only did my baby girl start to nurse—she ate like a woman with PMS tasting chocolate for the first time! (As a little side note, she did have a nursing problem: she would only nurse on my left side, which, of course, is the breast over my momma's heart.)

I was mesmerized as I realized I was holding the baby girl that I had always dreamed of but never thought I would have. I thought about the peculiar note that teenage girl had handed me weeks earlier. Finally, I realized that God wasn't punishing me; He was keeping His promise to me. I suddenly knew that God's promise was more powerful than any medical diagnosis. I was confident that Emmy was going to make it and thrive.

I had my girl and wanted to keep her close forever. As I was dreaming about our future together, I heard the Lord say to me in my heart, *I saved her life and set her apart for My Kingdom work on Earth. You will love her well, but you will have to let her go one day. I have called her to the nations.*

The minister in me felt honored because I knew I was raising up a world-changer. But my mommy heart was hurting because I never wanted to let her go. I actually named her after another woman who God sent to the nations, the missionary who led me to the Lord: Emily.

The next day, the doctor who had told me Emmy would be brain-dead came back into my room. It was funny because he told me that he was an atheist who didn't believe in miracles before saying, "I can't explain it, but all her tests that day came back normal. In fact, I re-ran her tests three times and even added new tests because I can't figure out how everything changed all of a sudden. But—" he paused and looked at me, amazed, "your baby girl has no more signs of any brain damage. Her hearing is also fine now. She passed the hearing test this morning, even though she seemed to have no response to it the other day. Somehow, all the things we were worried about before seem to be gone now. In fact, we will be able to release her from the NICU today. I have got to say, I'm a little bewildered. I have never seen a recovery like this since I've been a doctor."

I was crying tears of celebration as I said to him, "My God has done a miracle for me and my baby girl!"

"Yes, well, remember, I don't believe in miracles, or God for that matter."

Today my daughter is a very healthy, tenacious, twenty-one-year-old. Whether she's in the USA having coffee with a friend, finding homeless people to feed, or working, she is always about her Father's business. She changes the world every day because she is radically in love with Jesus. In fact, she loves Him so much that last year she put a backpack on and took a nine-month-long world mission trip with fifty others. She survived some of the most uncomfortable situations and saw some of the most heartbreaking things. But all of it gave her even more motivation to make everywhere she goes a mission field.

And yes, like God warned me, she does not live near me, but she does live every day for Jesus doing daily Kingdom work. We talk on the phone daily, and I always tell her that I gave birth to my best friend.

But the story of how God redeemed me from my shame doesn't end with Emmy's miraculous birth.

While she was still a baby, I was speaking once a month, and I would take Jake with me on the road so I could have time alone with him. There was such a big age gap between my two kids that I wanted to make sure Jake still had special time with his mom. After all, he had been an only child for eleven years. You can imagine how this little girl rocked his world. I remember looking at him and saying, "Eleven years from now, you could be married and having a baby of your own." As fate would have it, that's exactly what happened. My granddaughter, Olive True, is eleven years younger than my daughter Emmy.

Right after Jake turned twelve, I was invited to one particular event in Washington, D.C., for crisis pregnancy centers. Jake was excited to go with me. We had a great time on the plane, laughing and playing games. He was always fun and an easy child to travel with. He actually loved going everywhere with me to do ministry. When we got off the plane, we were greeted by the head of the crisis pregnancy center, who had come to pick us up at the airport. She said she wanted to talk to me about something once we got settled into our hotel.

As the bellman unloaded our luggage from her car, out of nowhere, she blurted out, "Sheri Rose, by any chance have you ever experienced an abortion? Excuse my boldness, but I feel like the Lord asked me to ask you that question."

I looked at Jake to see if he was listening. All I could think about at the time was that I still hadn't even shared about this part of my life with my husband, and my son certainly didn't know. When we made it inside the hotel, I asked Jake if he wanted to go to the pool and swim while the woman and I talked. He was excited and got himself ready really fast! While he was playing with some other kids at the hotel pool, I quietly and hesitantly told the woman about my experience and confided it was the first time I'd shared that part of my life with anybody since I'd become a Christian.

She said, "I know how you feel, Sheri Rose. It's got to be awful." She paused for a moment, then continued. "But would you be willing to share your story at the event tomorrow night? I believe it could help many of the young girls who are pregnant and contemplating getting an abortion. I also believe that if you will begin to share your story, you will be healed as you help others."

I thought about her request. How in the world could I share this in front of two thousand people? I hadn't even shared it with my husband, and I did not want Jake to hear it from me for the first time from a platform to an audience.

I glanced over at Jake. He was laughing and having so much fun in the pool with his new friends. The woman said she really felt like I needed to share. After a little more thinking, I told her I needed pray and ask God if I should share with Jake about my abortion before I made a decision, and then I would let her know.

All I could think about was Jake. I hadn't even had "the talk" with him yet, so I prayed hard. Then I remembered that his school was going to have a class on sex education as soon as we got back from this trip, so I saw that as God's opening the door for him to see the outcome of the "safe sex" that's pushed in public schools. I knew God was going to use it, but I didn't know how painful it would be for me to relive it and how painful it would be for him to hear it

When we got back to the hotel room, Jake was happy from having so much fun. "Mama, can I order room service?" he asked. He loved doing that when we were at hotels, and to be honest, so did I.

I'll never forget sitting there in the hotel with him fighting back tears as I began to explain to my twelve-year-old son that I got pregnant when I was sixteen and the doctor and my dad had talked me into taking the baby out of my tummy. But the hardest, most heartbreaking thing I ever saw were the tears Jake cried when he looked at me and asked, "Mama, are you telling me I have a brother or sister in Heaven?"

My shame was heart-wrenching as I held my son tightly and cried with him. "Yes," I replied, "and one day you will meet that brother or sister."

The next day, I felt it again. My past choice had me chained to shame. Jake was so sweet. He saw that I couldn't stop crying while I was getting ready to go speak, so he came over, hugged me, and said, "It will be OK, Mama. God will help us feel better soon." There's nothing better than childlike faith to comfort you when you're in an emotional crisis.

I had never been able to see how God could use my horrific story for anything good. But that night, when I got up on that platform and shared it for the first time, I got my first glance of His redemption of my mistake. I found out afterward that more than forty girls, ages thirteen to sixteen, in the audience had canceled their plans to have abortions after hearing my story. Instead, they chose life and adoption for their babies. I was blown away to think about the babies who were saved and the forty mamas who were somewhere praying for a child to join their family through adoption.

For the first time, I got to experience Romans 8:28 personally, which promises that "God causes everything to work together for the good of those who love God and are called according to His purpose for them."

While flying home from that event, I realized it was time to tell Steve about the abortion. When I did, he actually cried tears of compassion.

"You mean you suffered all those years by yourself?" he asked. Then he added, "I'm not mad at you, and neither is God."

I felt some relief, but I still had lingering shame and regret until one priceless Easter at the little church we attended in Sisters, Oregon. Even though I was a Christian speaker and I experienced so many beautiful things in Christ, for the first time that day, I understood why He went to the cross for my sins.

As our family entered the small, sweet sanctuary, the choir was singing about the old rugged cross. Ushers at the door were handing out big rusty nails and pieces of paper. Chairs had been set in a circle around a very rugged-looking cross with a purple robe draped over it. The pastor began to talk about Easter and the story of the cross in a way I'd never heard before. He talked about exchanging our chains at the cross for a changed life in Christ—a free and new beginning. As he spoke, I held that rusty nail so tightly that it discolored my hand. I've never seen a pastor share so passionately about bringing everything hidden in us into the light and truly receiving God's forgiveness. He opened our eyes to truly see the gift of repentance and what happens in our souls when we get naked and let our loving Heavenly Father wash our dirty sin and souls in the living water.

It sounded so good, but Satan certainly tried to stop me from going forward into my freedom. He knew if I broke free from his ugly stronghold of shame, I would carry this message of freedom to everyone who heard me speak and read every book I wrote.

Still, I lived in a small town; I couldn't help but wonder what people would think. Would I wipe out my witness for Christ by walking forward and nailing the secret sin to the cross? There was a spiritual battle in my head until I heard the voice of God whisper to me so tenderly, "This is why I sent My Son, Sheri Rose." Then I heard in my spirit, "This is between you and Me, My daughter. It's time for you to let Me free you once and for all from this chain of shame."

The next thing the pastor said gave me the courage to get up and nail my shame to the cross. "Don't waste the blood of Jesus wasting away in your sin." He invited us to take the nail we were holding and write the secret sin on the piece of paper. Then he said, "If you think your sin is too great for Jesus, then you're denying the power of the cross!"

Those words transformed my thinking, and for the first time, I cared more about what Christ did for me than what others thought about me. In that moment, I walked down to that cross, fell to my knees, and repented. I picked up the hammer that was provided, took the rusty nail from my hand, and pounded that secret sin to the cross once and for all as I declared the words of Jesus: "It is finished!"

That Easter, I could finally embrace and enjoy my children without fear. I finally felt like a new creation in Christ. There will never be a day that I will look back on that abortion and think it was a good thing. But there'll also never be a day I won't be thankful for what Jesus did for me on the cross, and I hold on to hope that I will meet my aborted child in Heaven, where we will be together for all eternity.

WHAT CAN GOD DO?

If you're dealing with an unplanned pregnancy and are not ready for a baby right now, I promise there's someone who can't have a child who is praying for one at this moment. You could be the answer to their prayers and give your child a chance at life with someone who is ready. I wish someone had encouraged me to have my baby and let someone adopt him or her.

I want to share a short story of a friend of mine. She had always been pure; she got married as a virgin to a really godly man, but about twenty years into their marriage, he walked away from the Lord, cheated on her, and left her.

She had always been a good girl, and she'd always loved God—one of those girls who really never did the wrong thing on purpose. She was raising three teenagers, and she set a high standard of purity for them. But one night, her pain got the best of her, and she ended up having sex with a man in a one-night stand. She got pregnant that one time—just like I did. But she decided to keep the baby, even though it was humiliating to have to admit to her teenagers and her church what she had done after she'd been so strong in her stance on purity. You can imagine the humiliation she experienced as a forty-year-old woman who was pregnant out of wedlock from a one-night stand.

But this woman had a best friend who had become like family to her and her kids—and this friend was unable to have a baby. So she decided to give birth and have her best friend adopt the baby. She and her husband had tried to have a baby for more than twenty years, and it never happened.

So God took my friend's poor choice, and when she gave Him the pieces, He created a beautiful family from them. That little boy is now six years old, and my friend gets to see him monthly when she gets together with her best friend. She says God gave her this to make her more compassionate for others who make mistakes or missteps. He used her good reactive choice to give her best friend her heart's desire. She also gave a boy a life to live and taught her three teenagers that one bad choice can be redeemed with a good choice to do the next right thing. I know she'll never look back with regret, and she doesn't live with the shame that I carried all those years.

What Can I Do?

Repent

I realize repentance is rarely discussed in church anymore, but if you don't repent, it's like getting in the shower every day and not turning the water on to wash away all the dirt. What good is a shower if you don't turn the water on? What good is soap if you don't use it? Repenting is a gift; it's a compassionate cleansing of the soul from the Lord. There's nothing more beautiful than getting your soul naked before God and allowing Him to do what only He can do to set you free from secrets and shame. If I had never repented and had continued hiding my abortion from my husband, I would have continued to walk in shame all of the days of my life. If I had stayed chained to Satan's secrets and shame, I believe you wouldn't even be reading this book right now, because I probably wouldn't be in ministry.

Be Compassionate, Not Condemning

I wasn't a Christian when I had my abortion. I wish I had known then that God had a better way for me. Maybe you're reading this right now and saying, "I would never do that!" Maybe you wouldn't, but sin is sin, and each of us is offered the same redemption from Christ. The best gift you can give to anyone is to show them His love and compassion. Think of His example when He knelt by the adulterous woman everybody wanted to stone. She had a bad reputation and had been caught having sex when Jesus came across her. In His gentle way, He addressed the angry mob, saying, "Let any one of you who is without sin be the first to throw a stone at her."

His Love Letter to You

My Beloved Daughter,

The greatest battle you may ever fight is the fight to forgive yourself. Remember, My beloved, all My chosen ones had to get up and receive My gift of grace to finish living out their faith. I gave My disciple Peter the strength to get up from guilt. I gave My anointed King David the grace to get up from the shame of committing adultery. I gave My apostle Paul the mercy to get up from pride and arrogance. I gave My warrior Gideon the courage to get up from his fears. The time is now to accept My forgiveness and finish what I have called you to do. Nothing can keep you down, because My power to rise again is in you.

Love,

Your Heavenly Father

"The righteous keep moving forward, and those with clean hands become stronger and stronger." (Job 17:9)

Chapter 5

Beyond the Trials of Motherhood

God, help me believe You are with me in these tears and trials.

Annie couldn't wait to be a mom. As a little girl, she'd been like another mom to her baby brother. She always told her mama, "Thank you for having this baby for me!" She always carried baby dolls around—feeding, burping, and changing them. Her mom talked a lot about adoption and told Annie about kids who needed families. Annie's young heart broke for them, and she told her mom, "When I grow up, I'm going to adopt all the babies that need a good, loving family!"

"You're going to need an orphanage, sweet girl, not just a home to do that," her mama said with a smile on her face.

Annie also dreamed about being a professional athlete, since she loved sports. One of her biggest dreams came true after she graduated from high school: she got a scholarship to one of the most prestigious colleges in Southern California to play volleyball. She couldn't believe God gave her that opportunity! She loved the volleyball team, the big football games, the excitement of competitions, and the liveliness of the campus. Her team was one of the best in the country, and she felt blessed and honored to be part of it. She's not the type who exalts herself, but she knew deep down that God gave her favor as a sort of celebrity athlete on campus—and of course, it didn't hurt that she was beautiful and kind. Annie loved the Lord and was the type of girl that used anything and everything to point to her Heavenly Father.

It looked like her life was going perfectly—until she injured her back terribly one day during practice. She was a tough girl and thought it was a simple injury that could be fixed with physical therapy. However, it got worse the next day, and her coach insisted that she get X-rays before he would let her practice again.

The doctor informed her that if she continued to push herself to compete at such a high level, there was a chance she could injure her back so badly that it could cause many long-term problems—including not being able to carry a child to full-term pregnancy. She prayed, "God, please just heal my back! You gave me this opportunity, now heal my back so I can keep going. I want to be part of my team and love them for You!" But God knew best, and Annie ultimately had to end her athletic career to retain her mobility—and hopefully, some day, to experience motherhood.

She was so sad. She felt lost as she continued through school without her team, so she decided to push hard and graduate early from college. Then she went home, disillusioned, and asked her mother, "Mom, am I crazy? I just gave up my athletic career, my scholarship, my social life...everything I loved for the sake of my hypothetical children and the hypothetical husband that I would have them with. The man I thought God told me I was going to marry dumped me out of nowhere, and I have no other potential husband."

"Well," her outgoing mom replied, "I can fix that!" Without letting Annie know, her mom signed her up for a Christian dating service. You can imagine Annie's surprise when she started getting calls from random guys who wanted to take her out. She thought God was playing a practical joke by giving out her phone number without her knowledge.

What she did not know was that He was about to bring back a young man, Todd, whom she had loved for years but who had dumped her two years earlier. She never thought she could actually have him for herself, mainly because every other girl wanted him, including her best friend. She told me that the very first time she saw him, she thought God told her Todd was her future husband.

She had met him in high school and had developed a great friendship with him. Then in college, when they finally had the chance to date, God whispered a promise to her: "This is the man I have made for you." But out of nowhere, Todd dumped Annie for one of her best friends. Not only was it heartbreaking for her, but it was almost impossible for her young heart to hold on to the promise she believed God had given her of becoming Todd's wife one day.

You can imagine her surprise when God opened up a full-time ministry job at the same Christian organization where Todd was volunteering weekly. I can see her surprised look as she walked in and saw his face for the first time in two years. She told me he had broken her heart so many times in the past that she actually thought, *Is this God or Satan that he's back in my life now?*

Todd had undergone a serious heart change toward Annie, and he was excited to see her. But he could see from the look on her face that he had a lot of making up to do if he was going to get her attention again. She still loved him, but she was scared and determined to guard her heart.

One day, he came into the office with her favorite flowers and her favorite chocolate bar. After he sweetened her up, he did the next sweetest thing. He looked at her humbly and said, "I know you don't want to hang out with me alone, but I set up a volleyball game this evening with some of our friends at our favorite beach. Would you at least come and play with all of us after work?" Well, that did it—her favorite beach, her favorite friends, and she missed volleyball so much. She couldn't help but say yes. Plus, in the weeks leading up to this gesture, he'd been acting as sweet as the chocolate he had given her.

He was a man with a plan that night: he was determined to show her his heart and win hers back. After volleyball, while she washed up in the bathroom, Todd set up a perfect sunset picnic dinner, complete with dessert and sparkling cider. When Annie returned, she was surprised to see that the rest of their friends had left. Todd politely asked if he could hold her hand. Annie's heart softened in that moment, and she couldn't resist.

Todd told Annie he had written her a letter he wanted to read aloud to her, and she could keep it afterward so she could remember his words and hold him accountable for them from that day forward. As he began to read, tears flowed down his cheeks. He apologized for everything he had ever done to hurt her and took responsibility for every action and reaction that had been wrong. When he was done, he handed her the letter, put his arms around her, and held her until the sun went down. Then he got down on one knee and told her he loved her for the first time. He said he had always loved her, but now he knew that he was in love with her and wanted to spend his life with her.

Annie was overwhelmed with joy, and as they stood there in silence for a moment, she told me she could hear the Lord whisper to her a second time, "I told you he was the man I made for you." She knew in that moment that God does keep His promises as He prepares hearts in His perfect time.

Once she settled into the fact that Todd was indeed the man God had prepared to be her husband, she let herself fall deeply in love with him again. Two years later, their wedding took place at the spot on the beach where Todd made everything right with her, and where he had later proposed. I guess you could call that "their spot." They had a picture-perfect wedding with family and friends, and they celebrated what God had done through their long journey to finally becoming husband and wife.

Their first night together was sweet and pure because they both had saved themselves for marriage. Todd began by removing Annie's sparkly wedding shoes and washing her feet. He wanted to start their marriage off by loving and serving her as Jesus had done. They prayed together and thanked God for their love for each other and His love for them.

All week while they were on their honeymoon, Todd and Annie talked about their future children, and Annie laughed, lovingly letting him know that she had already picked out names for each of them when she was seven years old, so it was set in stone before they met.

Annie was excited to start a family with Todd, so as soon as they got home from their honeymoon, she ran to her computer and registered to get them both certified for adoption. They both loved the thought of giving a family to someone who didn't have one.

In the meantime, they got pregnant with their first son. Prior to her pregnancy, Annie had wondered if God had given her a heart for adoption because she wouldn't be able to get pregnant or because her back injury had already caused too much damage for her to carry a child. As the enemy likes to use fears and lies to wipe out our joy, she had a continual fear that she would miscarry the baby throughout her pregnancy. It didn't help when other women would share their horror stories with her while she was pregnant. But not only did she not lose the baby, but she also carried him two weeks past her due date. (I guess her baby boy was comfy and cozy in there and didn't want to come out!)

When baby Derek, their pride and joy, was finally born, he was the most colicky baby anyone had ever met. He screamed, ate, screamed more, filled his diaper, screamed more, and repeated the process with little to no sleep in between. Annie would spend hours trying to calm and comfort him. After holding, snuggling, bouncing, walking, comforting, feeding, changing, swaying, and carrying him, he'd still be screaming. Eventually, she would get him to go to sleep, but the rest usually only lasted for twenty-minute increments before the cycle started all over again.

Annie wanted desperately for her baby to be well, but instead, things got even worse. At six weeks old, baby Derek broke out into a full-body rash. Annie went on strict diets for several months to make sure nothing in her milk was causing an allergic reaction, but nothing helped.

At three months old, Derek was still covered in the rash, and he scratched his arms and legs to the point of bleeding anytime he had bare skin exposed. No matter what Todd and Annie tried, poor baby Derek screamed and scratched relentlessly. Annie made homemade baby food and read books and medical journals about allergies, gut issues, eczema, colic, reflux, and every other issue doctors said might be plaguing him.

The happy couple who wanted nothing more than to start a family was now exhausted, exasperated, and hopeless. They didn't know how they would ever get to the other side of this.

Annie received endless advice from friends, family, and strangers alike. The devil whispered to her regularly, "You're terrible at this! Look at you! Everyone else around you can do this. Why are you so bad at it? Look at your baby. He doesn't work like anyone else's child. They seem to have it figured out. Clearly, you weren't cut out for this." The lies permeated her heart, and she began believing them.

She couldn't go anywhere with Derek. She tried to go to church and Bible study as he got older, but every week, he just screamed so much that she always ended up having to leave so other people could hear what was going on. The isolation became intense. Annie had always been an extrovert—people are what God used to help recharge her. But her usually bubbly demeanor began to wither.

She felt she had failed at being a mom—but she wasn't a quitter, so she kept striving. She held and loved her baby boy all day, every day. While she was in the hardest, most heartbreaking season trying to care for her first baby, the adoption agency called and said they had a baby for them. Once again she thought, *Is this God's timing or Satan's sick way of messing with me?*

All she knew for sure was that in that moment, her life was a hot mess, and motherhood, so far, was a complete disaster. How in the world could she bring another child into their family right then? But, as God has a strange sense of timing, she got pregnant with their second child during this crisis. She knew she had prayed for a big family, but a screaming sick baby, a second pregnancy, and the possibility of adopting a child at the same time seemed like drinking water from a firehose.

When she went into labor the second time, she had a little fear because the first delivery had not gone well. When Derek was born, he wasn't breathing and had to be rushed to the NICU, so she did not get the joy of holding him for a few days. Then, she could never put him down because of his screaming and his horribly itchy, rash-covered skin. You can imagine her relief when she heard the sweet sound of her second baby's cry as Todd announced with great joy, "It's a boy!"

This time, the doctor was able to put the baby right on top of Annie's chest while Todd cut the cord. Annie wrapped her arms around her son, smiling and breathing like an athlete who'd just finished a race. Her baby cried and looked at her. One eye was wide open while the other was squeezed shut. *Awww, what a cutie*, Annie thought. *He's already winking at me.* But soon there was concern in the delivery room: it appeared that one side of baby Brayden's face was paralyzed. The doctor said this sometimes happens in utero, but the paralysis would likely dissipate over the next month or so.

But several months passed, and baby Brayden's facial paralysis continued. The pediatrician told Annie he might have had a stroke in utero or that he could have a brain tumor and scheduled an MRI to find out. Annie was filled with thoughts of the worst-case scenario. Satan had a field day tormenting her every day until the test results came back. Praise the Lord—they were negative for both a stroke or a brain tumor.

Brayden was diagnosed with a rare neurological disorder, and his parents were told that his facial paralysis would most likely be permanent. But Todd and Annie were grateful; when you think your child might have something as serious as a brain tumor and then find out he doesn't, facial paralysis becomes a blessing by comparison.

Derek was then three years old and still suffering from gut issues, allergies, and skin troubles. Annie longed desperately just to be able to take her children to a playground and talk to other moms about the cute little things that toddlers do. But the few times she'd gotten the courage to go, she was accused of spreading Hand, Foot, and Mouth Disease, or other parents would grab their kids and pull them away from Derek, thinking his skin condition was contagious. It was heart-wrenching for Annie. She so badly wanted her son to be healthy, and she was tired of all of the judgment she encountered daily from other moms. She desperately wanted her son to feel loved—to see him smile, feel happy, and laugh like all the other children. Instead, he scratched, screamed, cried, and threw tantrums. He was always so exhausted because he still only slept in twenty- to forty-minute increments at night due to his intense itchiness.

As she prayed for him to find joy and someone to play with him, again God answered her prayer in an unexpected way.

One day, Derek said, "I want a sister now, Mama. Can you give me a sister?"

"That's so cute, Derek. But it doesn't exactly work that way, honey. We don't get to choose what God will give us. But you know we've always talked about adopting, and maybe one day God will give us a sister through adoption."

"Well, I don't care if we adopt her or if she comes out of your belly, but I want a sister."

"Ha, ha! I hear you, sweet boy. I can't promise you that I can get you a sister. But I will tell you this: God cares about what's on our hearts. So if you're really thinking about this that much, you should probably be talking to God about it."

"OK," Derek replied. At three, he sometimes displayed the understanding of an adult. "Dear God, could You please bring me a baby sister? I really want one. I don't care if she comes out of my mommy's belly or another mommy's belly. I just really want a sister. Amen!

"There, now I'll get my sister."

Annie chuckled. "Well, I didn't say you'll get a sister necessarily, but I love that you are talking to God about what is on your heart, sweet boy."

To Annie's surprise, Derek's prayers for a sister continued every night for weeks. Then, one morning when Annie woke up, she felt an internal nudge to take a pregnancy test. To her shock, two lines popped up immediately! The next day, Annie was in her bedroom when little Derek walked in. He ran up to Annie, hugged her legs, and put his ear to her belly.

"What's in there, Mama?" he asked as he rubbed her tummy.

"Huh?" she asked, totally caught off guard.

"What's in your tummy?" he asked again.

"What are you talking about, Derek?" Annie continued trying to hide what she knew—that there actually was a baby in her tummy.

"It's my sister! She's in there!" Derek said as he pulled his ear off her tummy and looked at his mommy with a sparkle in his eye. "I've been asking God, and He did it! He has my baby sister coming. She's in there!" he said with great childlike faith as he pressed his pointer finger against Annie's tummy.

"Oh, Derek, you're the cutest! I love you, sweet boy!" she said.

"I can't wait to meet her!" he said, and then ran out of the room filled with joy.

Annie was astonished. *What in the world was that?* she thought.

But Derek's unwavering faith struck her that day. It was the most beautiful thing she had ever seen. Still, fears of miscarrying haunted her, and then there was the obvious question. *What if this isn't a girl?* she thought. *I know there's a baby in there, but I don't know if it's a little girl. Oh my goodness, please Lord, don't let him down. Encourage his faith, God, please.*

Annie had no idea how her own faith was going to need encouragement too. The week they found out they were pregnant was also the week little Derek's body took a turn for the worse. His skin got dryer, thicker, and itchier than ever before. His body seemed to be reacting to everything. His sleeping got worse, which meant Annie didn't sleep at all. Days turned into weeks, and Annie and Todd were more exhausted and discouraged than ever. Annie worried that her stress and extreme lack of sleep would cause a miscarriage. She prayed daily, begging God to heal Derek, but sadly, he only got worse.

Annie's heart was breaking for him. Derek had become anxious. He asked questions before he touched anything for fear that touching something new could cause his already red, scratched-up, scabby body to further react. His little fingers crawled up and down every inch of his skin from head to toe constantly throughout each day. Annie tried everything to make him stop: gloves, Play-Doh, distractions, incentives, holding, cuddling, stories, clipping his nails every day. Nothing could keep his little hands from habitually ripping his own skin apart.

One night as Annie held back tears while watching Derek and Brayden in the tub, Brayden's pudgy arms splashed, and Derek's little hands scratched their way up and down his skinny, scabbed arms like a flutist playing scales on his instrument. As usual, he was miserable and tired from all of his sleepless nights.

"Oh, sweetie, I'm so sorry your skin is like this," Annie said. Her lip quivered. She felt so hopeless. He had suffered for almost four years, and after all they'd done, he'd only gotten worse. Annie still worried that he'd never meet the baby inside her. It seemed impossible that her body could withstand any more stress or sleeplessness. "I wish I could take your skin and put it on me so you wouldn't have to have this." She pressed her lips together and quickly caught the tear that forced its way out.

Derek looked up at Annie, his little hands still rapidly scratching. He'd moved on to his legs now, and the skin around his ankles was peeling off in the bathtub. She could see the skin floating and fresh specks of blood appearing and then quickly dispersing in the water. Derek's lower lip came out in slow motion. Annie could see that what she had said had triggered something in him. Then his puffy eyes squeezed shut and tears started coming out.

"No, Mommy, no!" he cried. "I never want you to have this skin. If you had this skin, it wouldn't help." Then he said what all toddlers who love trash day more than any other day would say: "Why can't we just take this skin to the dump and put it there? That way no one has to have it!" His tears dripped into the foggy tub. Annie leaned over and kissed his rough face as her tears dripped into the bathtub alongside his. She wished she could grant his wish.

"You're so smart, Derek. You're right! No one deserves this skin. I wish we could take it to the dump too, buddy."

"Can we?" he asked through sniffles.

"It doesn't exactly work that way. But we can keep praying," she said. With her arms wrapped around him, she said. "God, please heal my son. Please, Lord, we need Your healing hands on him so desperately. Please, Lord, help us."

Several more months of suffering passed. Ultimately, Derek's doctors told Todd and Annie he would need chemotherapy and laser skin treatments. After all the other medicines, diets, skincare regimens, and treatments had failed, this was their last option.

For years, Todd and Annie had begged God to heal their son. Now they changed their pleading and asked Him to just give them an alternative. In the midst of this intensity, Annie's due date arrived, and she gave birth to a baby girl.

Derek had newfound hope when his little sister arrived—after all, she was the one he had prayed for specifically. It was as if God was using her to remind them that He was good and He did answer prayers. God miraculously answered their prayer for an alternative treatment too, and despite being advised against it, the couple decided to try something unprecedented with their son. Within months, Derek's little body finally began healing. For the first time in four and a half years, Todd and Annie had hope that their agony, suffering, and exhaustion were turning around.

Within a year, Derek was completely healed. Todd and Annie were so grateful. The family spent another year getting used to being a family of five with three healthy children. When their daughter, Cory, was two years old and the boys were on a steady track of health, Todd and Annie felt they were finally ready to adopt.

Around that time, an adoption seminar was held at their church. The speaker shared about the three ways people go about it: international adoption, private adoption, and adoption through foster care. Though Annie had heard lots of stories that made her fear pursuing adoption through the foster care system, she and Todd both felt a tug on their hearts from the Holy Spirit and knew He was leading them down that path. In foster care, the goal is to help children reunite with their birth families; adoption only happens when every attempt to do so fails.

That night Annie began to play out all the possible scenarios she had heard about fostering. She pleaded with God, "Lord, I can love a hundred kids if You want me to. But I'm so scared to love one with all of my heart and have to say goodbye to them with no promise of ever getting to see them again."

She felt God whisper to her, "Will you love whatever child I send to you whether you get to keep them or not? Annie, ultimately they're all My children, including the ones you gave birth to. Do you trust Me with your family, Annie?"

After all Annie and Todd had been through already with their young family, one thing they knew was that they trusted God. Though they had struggled through a disillusioning parenthood up to that point, they had seen that God was with them every time their dreams were dismantled. They had experienced His peace and provision firsthand. Annie now knew that in order to see a miracle, you must need a miracle.

She felt comforted when Todd reminded her, "Listen, Annie, if God is leading us to foster care, even if we don't get to see the outcome here on Earth that we are hoping for, we will get to see it in eternity." She knew he was right. She had learned that sometimes the outcome on Earth wasn't the complete picture of what God was doing. They agreed that they wanted to follow God wherever He led, and now they knew He was leading them into foster care.

Annie and Todd had a new mindset: they would obey God's direction and love on hurting families even if it took them through personal heartbreak. Knowing little else, they dove headfirst into the foster care system and got certified.

They tried their best to ready their three children, ages six and under, to become a foster family. They knew this was a family endeavor in every aspect. They explained, "We will take care of each child until their family is ready for them. If a child comes into our home and it turns out that their family can't take care of them, then we would be happy to adopt them into our family forever." The kids seemed to understand and embrace their new roles as the older siblings.

Todd and Annie's first call for a child came days after getting certified. They were given almost no details except that the child was a five-month-old boy. They said their first "yes," and within days they met the social worker to pick up their first foster son. Upon looking through his paperwork and learning more about his case, they learned he was actually only three months old and that they would be his third foster family. They realized his case would probably take the maximum time and that he would probably remain in their home for twelve to eighteen months, but from what they could tell, it seemed clear he eventually would be reunited with his family. Annie thought, *OK, God, here we go. You gave me this heart to love, and now I need You to prepare me to love the way I want to, even though I know my heart will break when he leaves.*

When baby Jesse arrived, he didn't cry for the first several days. He didn't laugh, he didn't roll over—he really didn't do anything but sleep. Todd and Annie had learned about this in their certification classes; he was shutting down. Babies whose attachments are broken over and over will stop expressing their needs because they quickly learn that no one is going to meet those needs anyway.

But in his new home, baby Jesse was instantly smothered in love. He now had three older foster siblings who adored him and two parents who fell in love with him the moment they met him.

As a mom, Annie worried for her older kids. *Are their hearts going to break when we have to say goodbye? Will they hate me for letting them love someone who we asked them to accept completely, even though we knew that he would probably leave us someday?* The kids loved Jesse so well. The only thing she could do was pray and ask God to take all the worries and fears away. Only Jesus could walk them through every aspect of this dynamic and heart-wrenching scenario.

After two months of being with Todd and Annie, little Jesse's case had become the nightmare they had feared. It was every horror story they'd ever heard about foster care and then some. They felt scared, but they were committed to keeping him safe and working for reunification with his birth family, even if it took the maximum legal amount of time.

Suddenly, the case became volatile. Jesse's birth family began making threats against Todd, Annie, and the agency that had certified them. County officials grew concerned about baby Jesse's safety as well as the safety of Todd and Annie's family.

In the middle of a Wednesday morning, with Christmas just around the corner, Annie got a phone call from an unidentified number. As usual, her heart skipped a beat because unidentified numbers were always someone from Social Services. Annie answered, not knowing what was about to hit her. The conversation was brief, cold, and to the point: Annie was told that Jesse would be leaving their house on Friday to go to a new foster home, which would be kept confidential for safety reasons. She was told to meet the social worker in a particular parking lot to drop Jesse off and say goodbye.

Annie hung up the phone, numb. *How could I tell my kids? This is our worst-case scenario in foster care. I feel like a failure! Not only did we not provide a permanent home to Jesse, but we won't even get to see him reunited with his family. Oh my gosh, this poor baby is going to be sent to his fourth foster home in five months! Will he be okay? Will I ever get to know what happens to him?* Annie's thoughts blew through her mind like a raging hurricane.

For two days, their family continued to love a child they would soon know nothing about. It was a strange, surreal feeling. It felt like knowing the date of their child's death. Outsiders made comments suggesting they didn't have the right to feel grief or loss because he "wasn't their child" and "this is what they signed up for." It was a whirlwind of emotions that Annie mostly felt she wasn't allowed to have.

That Friday, they all woke up early and got baby Jesse ready. They drove about forty-five minutes to meet the social worker in a random, barren parking lot that felt like a desert wasteland. The social worker quickly grabbed Jesse from Annie's arms and hurriedly placed him in the back of his car. Then he buckled the worn-out car seat and slammed the door. He chuckled and said, "At least you only had him for two months." It took everything in Annie not to burst into tears and fall to her knees in the middle of that parking lot.

All she could think was, *No one would ever say that to a person who had just lost a child in any other circumstance. I get it, he wasn't "our" child by law. But we were asked to do a job of loving a child like he was our own, and we did it well. Today, we are being told that this child we love can no longer be in our family, and we just have to accept it without any questions asked.* Annie's heart pounded. She looked at her kids' faces, her daughter's quivering lip. They had no say in any of the matters, just a requirement to accept it. But they all deserved a goodbye.

Annie opened the social worker's car door and asked, "Can we say goodbye?"

He looked surprised. "Oh, sure. You want to say goodbye?"

Annie felt awkward but didn't care. She leaned into the car and kissed the baby she had kissed thousands of times in the past two months. She felt the social worker's eyes boring into her. The man was caught even more off guard when Todd and each of their kids took their turns reaching into the car to hug and kiss baby Jesse goodbye.

After the brief farewell, the social worker, hopped into his car and drove out of the parking lot. Annie strained to keep her eyes on baby Jesse in his car seat until she couldn't see him anymore. She worried that would be the last time she saw him. *He will never even know who we are or remember us,* she thought, *but our lives have been forever changed by this time with him in our family.*

In their short time as foster parents, they'd quickly learned that parenting in "the system" came with a lot of heart-wrenching work and no credit at all. Baby Jesse could have been with them for a year, eighteen months, or forever, but on that day, his story with them ended, and the rest of the tale was uncertain.

The family went home to an empty crib. Jesse's clothes were in the laundry, and an empty bottle sat in the sink from his morning feeding. Annie questioned God's motives. *Why did You place adoption and then family reunification on our hearts so heavily if You weren't going to allow us to be part of either of those things? This is the worst-case scenario, Lord! I feel like a failure—we did neither of the things we set out to do. I can't even worry about my crushed heart right now because I'm so worried my kids are crushed beyond repair. Will they ever want to do this again? Did we do this the wrong way, letting them love him so hard? Lord, how could You let this happen? We have done everything You have asked of us. Why did You not at least give us any of the desires You placed on our hearts? I'm so confused!*

That night, Annie tried to lighten the mood by watching some old-school Christmas cartoons with the kids. In one, a silent story was set to music. All the little children in it got to celebrate Christmas with their families, but one didn't have a family.

Six-year-old Derek snuggled up to Annie. "Mommy," he said, "I don't like this story." His lip began to quiver. "All the kids get to celebrate except that one kid—" He paused, and then the tears began to flow. "—because he doesn't have a family to celebrate with."

No sooner had the words escaped his mouth than he and Annie were both crying tears they hadn't felt allowed to cry yet. They cried for baby Jesse, but they also cried for all the other kids like him and the families walking alongside them who felt just like they did.

"Derek, this is exactly why we are doing what we did with Jesse. Every kid deserves a family, don't they?" Annie replied.

He nodded, and they sat and cried a little longer. In that moment, Annie knew her family wasn't done, even though she still didn't know what was to come or how God would restore any of that part of their journey.

That night, Annie and the kids said bedtime prayers. Like every other night, she prayed for each of her kids by name. Suddenly, two-year-old Cory stopped her. "Mommy," she said, "don't forget to pray for Jesse."

Every night after that, if Annie forgot, Cory reminded her to pray for Jesse. In that moment, God pressed on Annie's heart that though Jesse was no longer part of their physical family, he would always be part of their family in their prayers. She realized that maybe, just maybe, that was the only reason they got to have him for the time that they did. Her whole perspective changed on their loss when she knew he still needed them, whether he knew it or not. Thanks to Cory, their family has continued praying faithfully for him ever since.

In the first week of January, Todd and Annie got a message from a social worker asking if they were ready to consider another placement, and they decided that they were. Their hearts were still raw, but they knew it was part of the process. Right after New Year's celebrations, they said their second yes to an eight-week-old boy—Adam.

Todd and Annie had looked to God in prayer every step of the way in growing they family. But there were three particular things that had always weighed heavily on Annie's heart about her future children. She finally decided it would be better to just give them to God in prayer. In the first week of meeting baby Adam, God revealed that two of Annie's specific prayers had been answered. By the end of the first month, the third and final prayer was also answered.

Annie believed that God was promising them that, one day, baby Adam would be their son through adoption. But shortly after his arrival, his case took a steep dive into every crazy story and fear they'd ever had. God reminded Annie of a boy's name He had given them years earlier when they were pregnant with Cory. It sounded eerily similar to baby Adam's birth name, and she couldn't help but wonder if it could be a perfect name for him if they one day adopted him. God gave many in the Bible new names when they got a new life with Him.

After one particularly traumatic court date , Todd and Annie sat in their backyard, almost catatonic. The court was pushing hard for Adam to go back to his birth family, and because they were required to monitor visits between Adam and his birth family, they were the only people involved in the case who knew what was really going on in the home Adam would potentially return to. They could tell with certainty that if he went back, he would die.

Todd and Annie wondered how they could keep holding on to hope through this awful rollercoaster. It was terrifying, but God had provided so much and had answered so many of their specific prayers; that gave them the hope they needed to keep going. They continued to desperately cry out for Adam's life.

Shortly afterward, Annie felt a nudge on her heart to look up the name she felt God had given them for little Adam. She was shocked to find that the name was Hebrew, and the meaning was right there in bold letters: *God's Promise*. She could barely catch her breath. You see, the only other time she'd felt she'd had a promise from God was when He'd told her that Todd was going to be her husband. As you know, their journey to marriage was crazy—it took five years for the promise God gave her to came to fruition. But because of that experience, she knew God never makes a promise He doesn't keep.

Todd and Annie watched their three older kids embrace baby Adam in ways that were nothing short of miraculous. Cory, whom

Derek had prayed for, became like a mini-mommy to Adam, following in her mama's childhood footsteps. She acted with love and maturity beyond her years, constantly putting Adam's needs above her own. As Adam got older and started to walk and play, she'd follow him around, making sure his every step was safe. During bedtime stories, she would hold him in her lap with her arms wrapped around him and kiss his cheeks tenderly.

Sweet Adam had suffered through lots of trauma in the system, and as a result, he didn't talk until he was almost three years old—but his big sister made sure she translated his every need or want. She knew what every shrug, smile, and cry meant, and she was always spot on. At church, she'd go into his Sunday school class with him as his helper. "He wants his favorite bear," she'd say when he got cranky and couldn't communicate his wishes.

Having God's promise for Adam in their heart got Todd and Annie through the next three years of hell on earth. They spent more than a thousand hours monitoring visits between him and his birth family. They took him to countless doctor's visits, court dates, social worker visits, and endured hours upon hours of calls and meetings with attorneys, mounds and mounds of paperwork, and more. In court, they were lied about, falsely accused, and demonized. The harder it got, the more they needed to hold on to God's promise. They knew His promise was bigger than the potential tragedies that would paralyze them if they focused on the problems alone. Yes, it was horrible, but it strengthened their faith like never before. God kept showing them to trust Him through all the accusations and let Him be their defender. He reminded them that He would deliver baby Adam and their family through it all in His perfect time.

What Can God Do?

That promise was a lifesaver to hold on to when Todd and Annie were drowning in discouragement. God's tender mercy was like a comforting, raggedy old teddy bear that makes a child feel safe and soothed. You see, because God had changed their hearts to not just love the child but also love each birth family they walked with, their perspective was changed. They were able to see each birth family through a lens like Jesus's. It wasn't easy, but in God's strength, they did everything they could to show Christ's love to them. Throughout Adam's case, the birth family had lashed out at Todd and Annie in ways that were excruciating and cost their family a lot of time, pain, and energy. But when Adam's case finally turned toward adoption, God began a healing process they had never thought possible.

Where Adam's birth family was once accusatory, they instead became grateful for Todd and Annie's family. Where they had once lashed out, they instead began to praise, thank, and encourage them for the family they were to Adam. They became grateful for how Todd and Annie handled their persecution. Because Todd and Annie hadn't lashed back at them through the process and had trusted God to be their defender, when the case was over, there wasn't added wreckage to deal with from Todd and Annie's actions. Annie told me, "Today, I realize that we will never regret loving people, even the people who are most difficult to love."

After more than three long years of walking Adam through foster care, Todd and Annie finally went to court for one last hearing. This time, it was to confirm the promise that God had given them three years earlier. When the gavel dropped that day, Todd and Annie finally had the blessing that their *son* was legally recognized by the state for what they already knew him to be. Annie told me, "I'll never forget how we felt that day when the judge announced to me, my husband, and our three children that we were now Adam's new family. On one hand, I thought, *We have been his family this whole time*. But on the other hand, I just felt relief that God's promise had finally come to fruition and the battle for Adam's life was over."

On that glorious day, they witnessed something on Earth much like what God does when we say "yes" to being part of His family: adoption. A few weeks after the court date, when the final documents had been processed, Annie opened the mail to find Adam's new birth certificate inside.

On it was his new name—the name God had given Todd and Annie for him.

On the lines that read "Mother" and "Father" were Annie and Todd's full names.

The promise God had given them had finally come to fruition. The child they had prayed about for years, fought for, and longed to have as their own was finally safe at home.

Adam will never fully understand the battle that was waged for his life. He won't remember the trauma Todd and Annie's lives held for three years on his behalf. But today, Todd and Annie can look back and see that God used every trial (literally and metaphorically) to refine and train their family for His purposes.

Every night at bedtime, Annie and Todd pray for each of their children by name. And Cory's trained example has rubbed off: Adam, who is now three years old and never met him himself, is regularly the one to say, "Don't forget to pray for Jesse!"

What Can I Do?

Let Go and Let God

I know this is a cliché, but honestly, the only way to live is by faith. If we walk by what we see, we will suffer every day. If we walk by what we *think*, we will suffer even more because our thoughts are where the battle really lies. But when we purpose ourselves to let go and let God have what we cannot control, we find ourselves in a place of peace no matter what the trial may be. Faith really is the substance of things hoped for. God doesn't always give us what we want, but He gives us what we need for His purpose to be accomplished through our lives. Let go and let God! Give in to God's will and watch what happens when you set aside your own agenda. Your Heavenly Father can surprise you better than Santa on Christmas Day!

Trust God's Timing

Annie had to wait five years to marry the husband God had promised her. God had work to do in Todd's heart first. Without that time, he would not have been a good husband.

Let's say you've been waiting for a baby for a long time, and you finally get pregnant. If you take the baby out before the nine months is up because you want to hold it now, the baby will die; he's not ready for you to hold him yet.

Likewise, we often want to open the gifts God has for us before it's time. But in doing so, we ruin the surprise and His supernatural plans for us. One way to learn to trust God's timing is to live for what's in front of you today. *This* is the day He has made. What does He want you to do *today*? I know He doesn't want you to live for tomorrow because we're not even promised tomorrow. Today is called "the present" because it's a gift.

Listen for God's Voice

Many times, we think God's voice is the one we hear in our head and in our heart. But in Psalm 23, King David says, "I shall not want." God's voice is a peaceful knowing, not a desperate wanting.

God's voice is always confirmed in His Word. Scripture says that His people hear His voice for themselves. While God can use other Christians to confirm what you've already heard, they don't hear God *for* you. Be careful not to hang on to any promise someone may have given you with good intentions but which God never gave you Himself. It's heartbreaking to God when He gets blamed for not fulfilling a promise He never made because someone else tried to play God in your life. Be still long enough to hear His voice and then confirm what you heard in the Word.

Give God Your Dream

My dream was to be an ice skater, and I was very good at it. But when my parents divorced, my mom took me off the ice, and that dream was dismantled through no fault of my own. Fast forward to my first speaking engagement years later: I was in an arena in front of ten thousand people. Ironically, it was an arena where a professional hockey team played, and the stage was set up on top of the ice. I asked God why He had brought me to an ice rink, knowing that was my lost dream. Inside, I heard Him answer, "I could've given you *your* dream and put you *on* the ice; instead, I gave you *My* dream and put you *on top of the ice* to further My Kingdom on Earth."

Today, I'm a grandma, and if I had gotten my dream, at best I would be performing at "Grandmas on Ice". I would not have built a legacy of faith for my children. I'm so glad God did not give me my dream because His dream is everlasting. One good question to ask yourself if you're disappointed is this: "Would my dream have blessed anybody else besides me and my family?" Remember, we're here for so much more than ourselves. Let's dream big for God!

HIS LOVE LETTER TO YOU

My Beloved Daughter,

I want to set you free from holding on to anyone but Me. I know your heart, and I know how much you love those close to you. But you, My child, must remember that those you love ultimately belong to Me—not to you. I didn't give you those relationships to tear you apart or to control you through fear of the future. Because I love you, I am asking you today to trust Me with those you love by laying them down at My altar. If you will obey Me, I will bless you as I blessed Abraham for laying down his much-loved son on the altar. I know what is best because I created each of you.

This test of your faith is not for Me, My beloved warrior... it is for you. I want you to walk the rest of your days in complete freedom and not fear for those you love!

Love,

Your Heavenly Father

"Trust in the Lord with all your heart; do not depend on your own understanding." (Proverbs 3:5)

Chapter 6

BEYOND A DIAGNOSIS

GOD, HELP ME UNDERSTAND. I WAS HAPPY AND HEALTHY! WHY DID YOU LET THIS HAPPEN TO ME?

As many of my readers know, I have been fighting cancer for years—but this story is not about my battle with this disease. It's about two of the most courageous young girls I have ever met who crushed the weight of cancer by using it for Christ.

Years ago, when I owned a production company, one of the things I did was produce beauty pageants. I used the pageants as a ministry. My ex-husband, Steve, and I would actually spend a year with these girls doing community events; at the end, they would compete for the state beauty pageant title. I know some of you may be thinking, *How in the world can a beauty pageant and community service go together?* But since our young girls are so obsessed with beauty, it is actually a great way to get them to see that true beauty is their hearts for humanity and how they love and serve others in their community.

After a year of having all fifty girls volunteer at different events on the weekends, they would spend the final week in interviews and rehearsals to compete for the state crown. On the eve of the pageant, I would share my testimony of how I found Christ and invite them to ask Jesus into their hearts. You're probably thinking, *How did you get away with talking about Jesus?* Well, as the director of a beauty pageant, you might not be able to, but when you own the production company, there's no one to report to but God. And He's a great boss!

Once, a young girl named Jacqueline came forward with tears in her eyes to talk with me after I gave my testimony. She told me she had never known there was a God whose love she didn't have to earn by being perfect. Cautiously curious, she asked, "Is it really true that God loves me no matter what I've done or what I do?"

I could tell she had been given a very twisted version of who God really is and why He sent His Son for us. I asked her a bit about her parents and upbringing. She said she loved her parents but was very afraid of their rejection—that she'd let them down somehow, that they wouldn't love her unless she always did the right thing. She was afraid they would never support any of her dreams, including the one of being in a beauty pageant. So she hadn't told them about competing in ours. (She was nineteen, so she wasn't legally required to do so.)

I explained that God loved her so much that He sent His Son to die for anything she ever did or would do wrong. "God created you," I said, "and there's no way you could be perfect. That's exactly why He sent His Son. God doesn't see you through your sin. He sees you through the eyes of His Son, Jesus." I looked her in the eye and continued, "Jacqueline, salvation is a gift from God that you can't earn. He just wants to give you that gift because He loves you!"

Jaqueline was never allowed to receive gifts growing up in her religion. So when I asked if she wanted to receive the priceless gift of salvation from God, happy tears welled up in her pretty brown eyes. She was like a little girl receiving her first Christmas present. She got so excited that she jumped up and down, exclaiming, "Yes! Let's pray the prayer! I want the gift that God has for me!"

It was so beautiful to see how she expressed her excitement about salvation. She received Christ as her Savior in that moment. God is so fun; He will meet us anywhere we are! I laugh as I think about how Jacqueline secretly entered a beauty pageant, but became a real princess by receiving Christ as her Savior. In that moment, she became a daughter of the King.

Ironically, Jacqueline ended up winning the beauty pageant the next night. Today, she will tell you that the worldly crown she received that night pales in comparison to the crown of representing Christ. I wish I could say that after that moment, she lived happily ever after and God gave her the perfect life. But as you know, that is not how life goes.

Her first battle, of course, was facing her family. Because she became a Christian, they kicked her out of her church, out of her home, and out of her community. Her parents rejected her and told the childhood friends she had grown up with that they should have nothing to do with her, since she had left that religion.

For Jacqueline's entire year as a beauty queen, she lived with us, and we became spiritual parents for her. I knew what she felt like because I had lost my Jewish family when I became a Christian. At the time, Emmy had not been born, and our son Jake was only five. He absolutely loved having Jacqueline live with us. I knew this was a God thing because she got to grow in the Lord, anchor her faith, and became a princess warrior who shared God everywhere she went.

At the end of the year, she moved to Southern California, where she had always dreamed of living. She landed an amazing job with a huge restaurant chain there and helped open new restaurants all over the country. She got plugged into a great church and made new girlfriends who loved God as much as she did. Honestly, when she was twenty and twenty-one, she was living the dream. Yes, she missed her parents and was heartbroken not to have them, but she had a sense of being able to breathe freely for the first time.

While she was in California, Jacqueline found out her father was dying of cancer. She flew back to her home state when she heard he'd taken a turn for the worse and was likely just a week away from his death. She knew he would probably reject her, but she had to see him one more time. When she walked into the room where her father lay, she did her best to tell him about Jesus. She wanted him to go to Heaven with her so badly. Believe it or not, in his final hour, he received Jesus as his Savior through the very daughter he had rejected. She was so thankful to have that final goodbye, knowing she would see him again in Heaven.

Jacqueline met an amazing man, Paul, at work, and they fell in love. They had everything in common, including Christ as the center of their lives. One night, in front of everybody at work, Paul proposed to her. He stood up on the table and told the whole restaurant that the girl he was going to marry was in the room. Everybody applauded as he got down on one knee, and Jacqueline said yes!

She was sure they were going to live happily ever after. Every day, she would talk about their plans together and what they were going to do to further God's Kingdom through their marriage. All Paul ever talked about was Jacqueline. They seemed to have an amazing relationship. Paul worked at the corporate office in Dallas, Texas, so she would have to leave beautiful, sunny California to marry her man. She decided it was worth giving up the beach for her boy and best friend.

A week before the big move, Jaqueline decided to fly in early to surprise Paul. They had already picked out a beautiful apartment together where they would live once they were married. Jaqueline let herself in, not knowing Paul was there. Sadly, upon entering their room, she found him asleep in their wedding bed with another woman.

Her heart was ripped to shreds. Jaqueline simply sat in the corner of the room until both of them woke up. You can imagine how freaked out Paul was when he awakened to see Jacqueline sitting there staring at him while he snuggled with another woman in their bed. Jacqueline bolted out of the apartment, and he ran after her. He begged her for another chance, but she knew if he was cheating on her when they were only engaged, their marriage would be a disaster.

She cried out, "God, we haven't even slept together! I can't believe he slept with another woman!" Jaqueline hailed a cab and jumped into the first one that stopped. She took her broken heart and flew back to California to get some healing with her girlfriends.

She had so many questions for God. She felt like she had been so faithful to witness to her father and withstand the rejection of an entire church and all her childhood friends in order to follow Christ. She wondered, if God loved her, how could this happen? She was in such agony that she had to quit her job. The thought of having to call off her wedding and let everyone know their relationship had fallen apart was more than she could bear. Jaqueline slipped into a deep denial, which soon led to a dark depression.

Just when she thought it couldn't get any darker, everything exploded. Jacqueline felt a lump in the center of her chest, so her friends took her to the doctor to get checked. She was perfectly healthy and had always taken good care of herself. She was sure it was nothing, but she wanted to get it checked out, just to be safe. In her wildest dreams—or, should I say, her worst nightmares—she never would've expected the diagnosis to come back as Stage Four cancer. She was grateful to have her best friend with her when the doctor said, "You have a tumor the size of a grapefruit in your chest cavity. I'm sorry to tell you this, but you have a very slim chance of beating this type of cancer. We can try chemotherapy and radiation, but I cannot make any promises at this point."

Those words triggered her. She remembered what cancer had done to her father, and now it was going to do the same to her. News spread quickly among her friends, co-workers, and neighbors. Jaqueline's condo looked like a florist's shop. She felt very loved and supported for the first time, and she knew her friends were truly the hands and feet of Jesus. God made sure she was surrounded with the love of His family because hers was not there for her.

God gave her a doctor with candid compassion. He talked to her directly and discussed the fact that she had a slim chance of survival because of how aggressively the cancer was moving. The doctor said, "But look, Jaqueline, that doesn't mean there's no hope. We will start with the most aggressive form of chemotherapy after the weekend. Once we shrink down the tumor, we will continue with radiation."

"I have one very important question left for you, doctor..." She hesitated for a moment, then asked, "Will I lose my hair?"

As a former beauty queen, so much of Jaqueline's confidence was tied to her hair. And she had *big* hair—Texas beauty pageant hair.

Her doctor answered, "Yes, Jacqueline, I'm sorry to tell you, but there is a 100 percent chance that you will lose all your hair." Then he looked her in the eye said, "I am so sorry to tell you this, sweet girl. Not only will you lose your hair, but you're going to lose your ability to have children in the future as well."

Jaqueline's heart fell into her tummy as tears of terror slid down her cheeks. She felt like everything in her life was dismantled from this disease and her dreams were dying faster than her body.

The doctor looked at her compassionately and said, "Jacqueline, I wish there was time to freeze your eggs, but we have to start chemo in two days. If we delay any longer, I don't believe there will be any chance for you to beat this cancer."

Jaqueline's girlfriends, who had accompanied her to the appointment, walked over and held her while she cried. One of them jokingly said, "Jacqueline, I'll have as many babies as you want to have. I'll be there as a surrogate mother if you'll beat this cancer for us!"

She went home after that appointment and tried to process everything she had been told. It hit her like a ton of bricks when she realized she would have months of painful processing during treatments and would only have two days to go play before the chemo hell began. So her friends took her to get her nails done. Next, they went to dinner at her favorite restaurant overlooking the ocean. The following day, they went to the beach and completed the weekend Sunday at church.

During worship, Jaqueline fell to her knees and begged God to heal her. She had so many dreams for her life, and she wasn't done yet. She wanted another chance for God to bring her a husband, a family, more time with friends, more time to impact lives. "Please God, stop this from happening," she begged over and over. She hated this.

Jaqueline woke up the next morning knowing it would be the last time she would feel physically strong for a while. She expected it to be hard, but she didn't know how hard it would be. She was petrified about this first chemo session, so once again, she brought friends for support. As they walked into the doctor's office, she looked around at all the other patients. The first thing she noticed was that they were all much older than her. She'd processed many different emotions by then, but for the first time, she started to feel alone in this battle. She so desperately wanted to be able to connect with someone her age who was going through the same thing, but she never did.

Jaqueline didn't know she wouldn't get to do chemo alone, in a room with just her friends. No, chemo was done in a large room with a bunch of La-Z-Boy-recliner-type chairs. Everybody being treated in the big "chemo room" got what they called "chemo cocktails" attached to them through IVs. The only good thing about the chemo room was that it overlooked the ocean, so that was a gift from God.

Jacqueline was surprised to find that every time they changed the kind of chemo, it did something different to her body for the whole of that cocktail. For instance, one kind made her eyes constantly move back and forth, almost like they were spazzing. Another made her instantly vomit into the little trash can placed next to every chair for just such an event. When treatment was over that day, she was exhausted and exasperated—and it was only Day One. The only thing left in her that was strong was her will to win.

Jaqueline told me it was lonely, but she discovered she was not alone because she connected with Jesus in a deeper, better way than ever before. She said that God became tangible to her in those days, and she could feel His tender touch with every tear she cried. She could hear His whisper as she walked her trial out with Him, one day at a time. Death's door opened her eyes to a real Jesus, and He became her best friend, her confidant, her healer, her provider, and *exactly* what she needed to survive her season of sickness.

After each appointment, she waited to find out how her body was going to respond to the chemo cocktail once she got home.

After her first treatment, she seemed to be tolerating it better than she expected. Then, in the middle of the night, it hit, and it hit hard and fierce. She spent several hours later that day and night violently throwing up. She had the most severe bone pains. It felt like someone was hitting her lower back with a baseball bat. At that point, the mental battle started in. Was this how it was going to be for who knows how long? She worried about her poor roommates. They didn't ask to have a cancer patient in their home. She knew this would change their lives as she became sicker and weaker. But then God reminded her that He put those special people in her life to care for her. She felt a peace knowing that He would carry her through the journey no matter the length of the battle.

Two days after her first chemotherapy session, Jacqueline got out of the shower and sat in front of the mirror in her bedroom to brush her hair. She was having a better day. The vomiting had dissipated, and the bone pain had decreased as well. As she pulled the brush through her hair, she could see it coming off her head in clumps. "It's happening! Why, God?" she screamed out loud, and her roommates came rushing in. They sat with her as she cried and panicked. She couldn't bear to pull out any more of her own hair, so she put down her brush and made an appointment with her hairdresser that afternoon to cut it all off. She thought maybe it wouldn't feel as traumatic if it was shorter.

Her sweet hairdresser cried with Jacqueline as she tried to cut her hair into a cute pixie, only to find it just kept falling out. Jacqueline covered her face with hands. She didn't want to see herself in the mirror, "Just shave it," she finally said. "It's all going to be gone soon anyway. What's the point?" She was so defeated.

That was the last day Jacqueline looked in a mirror for a long time. She felt ugly and unsure of herself for the first time. *How will I ever find a man to love me better than the one I had? He cheated on me even when I was beautiful. Who would want me looking like* this?

Jacqueline knew that she wouldn't be able to actually have babies, but now she wondered if she would even be alive long enough to adopt. The loss of her hair was the beginning of Jaqueline's loss of control. She became angry with God. "Why, God? Why?" was the question she found herself asking Him constantly.

After her hair came out, she didn't leave the house very often. The beach was her favorite place, but she wouldn't even go there because she might see someone she knew, and the thought of that was mortifying to her. Once treatment was underway, Jaqueline spent most of her days just lying in bed and watching TV—anything to numb how she was feeling. Whenever she used the restroom, she would make sure not to turn on the light. She kept her head down to avoid seeing herself in the mirror. She was repulsed by what the cancer was doing to her body and didn't want to see the evidence of it.

One day, a dear friend offered to take her wig shopping. She prayed God would help her find a wig that looked like her previous hair. After walking through several aisles of the store, she saw it! It was the same color as her hair, and a little longer than it had been.

But it was the name of the wig that sold her: It was called the "Delilah."

And so the adventure began. Having new hair brought Jaqueline some new hope. There were many adventures with Delilah, so many that she could write a whole book full of them. If Instagram had been around, she would have had a "Delilah" hashtag *for sure!*

In an effort to raise her spirits before her next chemo appointment, Jacqueline's friends decided they should all go to Knott's Berry Farm on a total whim. Yep, that was exactly what Jaqueline needed: a thrill-filled day where she could act like everything was normal. So Delilah was put on, and out they went. Jacqueline loved roller coasters, so they went on every single one.

When they got to the biggest wooden rollercoaster in the park, the real fun started. They stepped into their car, had their safety bars locked down, and off they went, up and down, so fast and so fun. By the end of the ride, Delilah had gone completely sideways and almost come off! Jacqueline's friend Nicole looked at her, and the two of them laughed for days. Laughter truly was the medicine she needed.

For many weeks, unless Delilah was on her head, Jaqueline continued to avoid the mirror. But one day, it happened. She caught a glimpse of herself without her wig. She saw a gray, puffy-faced, skinny girl, and she just stared and cried for what seemed like an eternity in that bathroom.

But as she stared at herself, she felt God more in that moment then she had in her entire life thus far. It was almost as if He were standing there with His arms wrapped around her, comforting her.

Suddenly, she felt an invisible touch, as if He were holding her face in His hands with her eyes staring into His. She heard Him say, "You have never been more beautiful, My daughter. Your hair and your earthly body are not what define you. Your heart and your love for others and for Me are. I have sent all these beautiful people to care for you. As much as you think you are a burden, there is always a blessing in what we think is a burden. Use this time to be a blessing." She will never forget that moment, ever. From that moment on during her cancer journey, everything that once was heavy or hard became joy and light.

Believe it or not, she beat all the odds and defeated the cancer. God redeemed everything even better than before, including providing her with a better man to marry. She let her husband know she couldn't have children, but he loved her so much she said he didn't care. He was excited to adopt children with her. Then God showed off even more. Jaqueline not only got pregnant once, but after her first baby, she even got pregnant again! She has two beautiful, healthy children—one daughter and one son. Even though she never got close to her own family, God gave her a spiritual family at her church and a beautiful community to live and raise their children in. She says that even on her hardest days, she remembers where God brought her from and what He did for her in her darkest season.

She's a crazy, all-raw-food, ketogenic dieter now. She hasn't had a sweetener in twenty years. After beating cancer, she went on to win the Miss California title, then got to compete in the Miss America pageant and tell her story to the world. She says that every day is a gift, and she intends to use that gift to show people God's love. I have to testify that she does it well and has one of the best attitudes of anyone I have ever met. No matter what she's going through, she always sees the cup as half full or, as I say, through Heaven's eyes!

WHAT CAN GOD DO?

I know many of you reading this story right now are saying, "That's a great story, Sheri Rose, but I lost someone I love to cancer, and they obviously weren't healed." Maybe God didn't heal your cancer, and like me, you're still fighting. So I want to show you how God works in so many different ways. Let's not forget that our lives are meant to be lived for eternity. He gives peace that passes understanding, and He puts purpose in our pain to draw us closer to Him and to draw others into eternity with Him. I've learned that faith is not what you say; faith is what you survive. I pray that this story of another young, beautiful girl who was diagnosed with cancer will really give you a perspective of eternity and why we are here on Earth.

I had the privilege of knowing a young girl named Sarah. When she was thirteen, doctors told her cancer would take her life within eight weeks. Her mom asked if I would pray with her. To be honest, all I could think was, *God, please heal her. She's too young to die.* My heart was fixed on the here and now, but Sarah's heart was fixed on eternity. When I called Sarah to minister to her, she ministered to me instead. She rocked my world with the way she processed her cancer diagnosis.

I asked, "How can I pray for you, Sarah?" Her response will forever be engraved on my heart.

"Sheri Rose, would you pray that before I die, I can share Jesus with my entire high school?"

With tears in my eyes, I prayed on the phone with Sarah that God would give her her heart's desire. In all honesty, all I could think about was, *I've lived for God's promises more than for His purpose, and the only thing she is living for is divinely driven by her eternal purpose. Wow!*

I wanted a cure for her cancer, and she wanted a cure for her friends' sins so that they could go to Heaven with her. It isn't a surprise that her name was Sarah, which means *princess*; she knew she was a daughter of the King. She knew her health didn't define her—her heart for her Heavenly Father did.

All day, I reflected on her heart for humanity. Sarah cared more about the eternal lives of others than her own earthly life coming to an end. Sarah had an eternal perspective, and she was committed to representing her King and sharing His truth—despite her circumstances.

The doctors gave Sarah eight weeks, but God gave her three years to live out her purpose and represent Him on her high school campus. On her sixteenth birthday, she announced in her peaceful, passionate, sweet voice, "I am ready to go home to be with the Lord. I know I have finished what He sent me here to do." Sarah's cancer had given her a unique and hard-to-ignore voice on her school campus. Her teachers and fellow students could not understand why this dying girl cared more about their eternal lives than her own.

As the end of her life drew near, Sarah was so weak. She was in a wheelchair but still insisted on going to school every day to love on people. When she knew she was coming to her final days, she asked a friend to push her wheelchair into the school office so she could speak to the principal. Then she respectfully said, "Is there any way you could let the entire high school come to my funeral? I wrote a letter for them that I want them to hear." She was so sweet, God gave her favor, and her principal said yes.

A few days later, Sarah was in her hospital room. It was her final day on Earth. I was there watching her mom thank God for every day she'd had with her daughter. She was telling Sarah, "You get to meet Jesus today! I love you, sweetheart. I'll miss you so much. But Heaven is going to be so amazing, honey."

I am a mom, but I don't think I could ever talk about Heaven that way if I were hurting the way she was. Her daughter had clearly rubbed off on her, and she had an eternal perspective. God gave her mom a gift that day. Just before Sarah drew her last breath, she sat straight up and said, "Jesus!" Her mom knew she was in the presence of her Savior.

The next day, Sarah's mom went to her school to meet with the principal and ask if he would keep his promise to her daughter. The principal made buses available during school hours for anyone who wanted to attend Sarah's memorial service. I had the honor of being there, and the church was completely packed. I rejoiced as busloads of teens from a wide range of backgrounds got off of those buses and entered that church. It was one of those miracle moments that God orchestrated for His beloved daughter Sarah.

He answered what seemed like an impossible prayer request because of her faith and her Heavenly Father's love for all the kids in that high school. From Heaven, God had given a voice on Earth through the letter she wrote before she went home to be with Him. As everybody was entering the church, the choir was singing, and this line of the song was repeated: "Soon and very soon, we are going to see the King!" Everyone at the service, including the many high schoolers, were actually celebrating Sarah's forever life.

Sarah's parents got up and tearfully thanked everybody for coming to celebrate their daughter's life with them. Then they asked the pastor to read Sarah's letter, which read:

Dear friends,

Please do not be sad for me today, for I am in a place where there is no more sickness, no more death, no more pain, and no more tears. I am in Heaven, and I asked God to open your heart to His love so that I will see you all here someday too! Then, we will celebrate in eternity together. My Savior, Jesus Christ, has made a way for all of you to get here! All you have to do is repent to Him for anything you have done and receive Him in your heart. He will forgive you forever and help you through the rest of your life like He helped me. Please pray today so it will happen!

Love,
Sarah

When the pastor finished reading Sarah's letter, he said, "If anyone here wants to stand up and say the prayer to receive Jesus, please do so now." At first, it was silent, and no one stood. Then those who knew the Lord began to pray for the kids silently. One stood up, then five, then ten more. By the time the song was done playing, more than three hundred kids were standing to give their lives to Jesus that day. God answered Sarah's heart's desire because it aligned with His desire that all will come to know Him.

The pastor then invited anyone who needed prayer to come forward. There were many church members there to pray with the kids. It was glorious to watch all those kids go forward. They were crying tears of repentance and recognizing they could have a better life than living for themselves.

I'm so thankful that Sarah lived driven by eternity so that they could be saved. One of God's precious children had cancer, and she used it to lead hundreds of people to her King. I wonder how many of those students went home and told their parents about Jesus. I wonder how many will grow up to become spiritual leaders in their homes, or perhaps even pastors, teachers, or evangelists.

GOD DETERMINES OUR FINAL DAY

I know death is so hard. The Bible says it is appointed to man to die but once, and God is the One who will decide when that day comes. So I want to say for those of you who did not have a loved one healed, I believe it was their time to go home to be with the Lord. They are now in a place where there's no more sickness, no more sadness, and no more pain.

I personally have been fighting cancer for over four years, and God has not healed me yet. But He has used the cancer to keep me very close to Him and to help me treasure every day as a gift. I believe He can heal anyone at any time. But I also know that He is sovereign. He knows the time we are going to be born, and He knows the time we're going to die. For those of us left behind, it's heartbreaking to lose someone we love. But those we love who are in Heaven are celebrating! One day, our forever life will begin, and when we get there, we will never have to say goodbye again.

What Can I Do?

Ask Yourself Hard Questions

What will I be remembered for when I am gone?

What have I contributed to the lives of those I love?

What effects do my actions or reactions have on my witness for Jesus?

The way we live today determines the legacy we will leave behind. If you are a Christian but have never specifically asked God to use you to further His Kingdom, take a moment to ask Him now. You'll be surprised what He can do with a life that is surrendered to Him. He loves you, and He wants to use you to change the world one person at a time. Don't miss your opportunity because of your opposition. You can rise above it in Jesus's name and use whatever you're going through to bring glory to God!

Don't Give Up on God

There was a famous Christian surgeon who knew how to do surgeries no one else could do. As a result, he saved thousands of lives. One day, he got a spinal disease, and it caused him to be paralyzed from the neck down. Still, he was determined to continue in his purpose. Some of his best friends set up a monitor on the ceiling above the bed he was bound to. He had headphones with a microphone in them and a camera on the ceiling. Believe it or not, this famous surgeon talked to doctors all over the world and coached them step-by-step through live surgeries. By doing this, he continued to save even more lives than before! With other doctors being his hands and feet, he was able to multiply the surgeries he did and train others. He led surgeries five hours a day, five days a week, and saved many lives. He also saved his own life as he realized that God used his limitations to teach doctors all over the world. Don't give up on God! While fighting cancer, I have written three books, including the one you're reading right now. I do videos from my home that reach the world for Christ. Nothing can stop God's purpose for you—not even the devil's diseases!

Live Every Day as If It's Your Last

Because one day you're going to be right. The only thing that matters is the here and now. Love whoever God puts in front of you. Let Him use you, and let Him minister to you personally today because that's all you have. The reality is that there will be a day you get to go home to be with the Lord. Death is the door that leads to a beautiful, everlasting eternity.

His Love Letter to You

My Beloved Princess,

You begin and end with Me.

You need not worry when your life will end, My precious child. All you need to know is that your first breath began with Me, and your last breath will lead you to My presence. Don't ever let fear of death or eternity frighten you. Your todays and tomorrows are secure with Me—I have held them in My hand since the beginning of time. When you finish your brief time on Earth and I call you into My presence, your forever life in Heaven will begin. But for now, My chosen one, you must live free from fear. Instead, trust Me to take you through every trial that comes your way. Remember that nothing in the universe can separate us. I am with you always...even until the end of time. So live well and finish strong—fixing your hope on the day that we will meet face-to-face on the other side of eternity.

Love,
Your Eternal King

"I am the Alpha and the Omega, the First and the Last, the Beginning and the End." (Revelation 22:13)

Chapter 7

BEYOND TEMPTATION

GOD, HELP ME WALK AWAY FROM WHAT I WANT AND TO DO WHAT'S RIGHT BEFORE IT'S TOO LATE.

The first time my dad saw my mom, it was through the window of the candy store she worked at across the street from the radio station studio where he was a DJ in Hollywood. My mom was stunningly beautiful. My dad was not nearly as good-looking, but he had a gift of words and an amazing personality. At the time, he was the youngest Hollywood disc jockey on the air. He used to joke that he was on radio because he had a face only his mother could love.

When my dad saw my mom for the first time, he had to meet her. That day, he went into the candy shop and made up a story to capture her attention. He told her he had been sent to Earth to bless her, but he only had one year to live. She laughed hysterically and replied, "Wow, that's the best pick-up line I have heard yet! How would you like to bless me?" They both started cracking up, and he knew he had gotten her attention.

What he didn't know for the first several months of their fun dates and flirting was that my mom was twenty-six years old, married to someone else, and already had two children. She didn't know my dad was only nineteen, just out of high school, and still lived with his parents. They both hid their ages and real-life situations from each other. I guess Hollywood was the perfect place for their hidden, hyped-up relationship, denying reality to live out their fantasy.

My dad was crazy about my mom. He loved staring at her stunning beauty through the window of his radio studio while she worked at the candy counter. As soon as he finished his live show every day, he would run to the flower cart and take her a bouquet. Then he'd wait for her to get off work so he could surprise her with another adventure.

My mom was the eye candy my dad craved. My dad was the romantic man my mom wished she had married. She wondered if he would ever run out of adventures and energy, but she loved every minute of it. They fell deeply in love and felt they couldn't go a day without seeing each other.

My dad and his father were best friends. My grandpa had just had a stroke, my grandmother was extremely ill, and my dad was the only child left to take care of them. My great-grandpa was an Orthodox Jewish rabbi from Russia who escaped Communism to get our family to America. His family was tightly knit together by their Jewish heritage and traditions. My dad had promised his parents he would never marry outside of the Jewish faith.

But my mom was not Jewish.

My dad knew his parents would freak out if they found out he was falling in love with a Gentile. (What if they'd found out that, besides not being Jewish, she also happened to be married to someone else?!) My dad didn't want to lose her, but he also didn't want to hurt them, so he kept their affair secret until they got pregnant with me.

Ultimately, my mom left her husband to marry my dad. Sadly, because the foundation of their relationship was birthed out of adultery and dishonesty, even after their marriage, she continued to have affairs with other men. Finally, he came to his breaking point, and my parents divorced.

So I witnessed firsthand the wreckage of unfaithfulness in a marriage and the horrific heartache that goes with it. I was determined to commit myself to fidelity and faithfulness when I grew up. (As you know from the introduction to this book, my husband and I ended up divorced for many different reasons that weren't unfaithfulness, but that's another story.)

What I'm going to share with you is something that happened to me twenty-five years ago during my marriage. I was twenty-nine years old at the time. Had the event played out the way it was headed without God's interventions, it could have destroyed my ministry and another family for the sake of temporary happiness here on Earth. The story could be a Lifetime movie of the week. So, if you like girl talk and supernatural escape stories, you might want to grab a cup of tea and settle in as I tell you this one. Please try not to judge me too hard as I share my heart and temptations with you. I'm not proud of this story, but I am proud of the outcome, so I feel it's necessary to share all the details so you can see how Satan sets us up. Even with the best of intentions, an unguarded heart can make catastrophic mistakes.

As you read in my earlier chapter on cancer, Steve and I used to own a production company. I produced beauty pageants and modeling and acting showcases all over the country to find new talent. Back then, we didn't have television shows like *The Voice* or *Dancing with the Stars*. What we had was a production company that was unique at the time because people didn't have to go to Hollywood to be discovered; I would bring the top Hollywood casting directors and agents to them. The production company became so popular that thousands of people would audition, but we would only take the top one hundred. We would spend a week with them in workshops, photo shoots, and classes, preparing them for their auditions and interviews with the agents and casting directors.

When I married Steve, he joined my production company and worked with me for a season. To be honest, this turned out to be very hard on our relationship. We did not work well together, but I felt obligated because he wanted to work with me. Because he was my husband, I wanted to honor him, and because we were Christians, we used the showcases as a platform to share our faith and lead many future actors and models to the Lord. So I put my marriage needs on pause and focused on the ministry.

But soon, I began to feel very lonely in my marriage, and the joy of the production showcases was fading fast. I could see that working together was actually destroying our love for one another. We became bad business partners and were no longer marriage partners. One day, I asked Steve not to work with me so we could save our marriage. I suggested he go get a job since he had two college degrees. He was so talented, I didn't think it would be an issue. But he refused.

Everyone who worked with us could see my joy diminishing. Soon, I lost all my passion for producing showcases. It began to feel more like a death sentence because everything in me was dying, including my marriage.

Steve became very frustrated and felt like a failure. I felt hopeless, heartbroken, and hormonal because I was pregnant with our first child. But we continued our work. During one particular showcase in California, a man named Matt came to audition and made the cut for the modeling category. He was an incredibly nice guy, and everyone adored him, including Steve. Matt was thirty-three, which is usually on the older side for a modeling career. But he was so dynamic and good-looking, he ended up beating out all the younger men.

After getting to know him throughout the process, I sincerely wanted to see him come to know the Lord. I could see that he had a good heart but didn't know our good God. After he won the competition, he said he was so touched by the way we ran everything that he would be honored to help out at any future events at his own expense.

Matt lived in San Diego—where my father also lived—and made a lot of money through his own successful company. He had enough good employees for the company to run itself while he was gone. I honestly think he tried out for the showcase just for fun and never expected to win. But God had another plan. He cared about Matt's soul being saved, and He used something fun to lead him to a life of faith.

I never said anything to anyone at the production company about my marriage. I felt like I needed to cover in order to protect Steve and be respectful. But my friends and family could see I was silently suffering. Many of them grew very angry toward Steve, which did not help our marriage.

Matt thought we had a great marriage because that's what I portrayed. Matt was mesmerized by our ministry and said he would come to the showcase even if it was just to watch me love people. Of course, my heart was touched, but I thought nothing of it at the time. My only thought was that I was thankful to get to show Matt the love of Jesus when I loved others.

Steve really connected well with Matt. To be honest, Matt became a good buffer between me and Steve; he was so refreshing to be around that when he was with us, we stopped fighting. He was a blessing who brought joy back to our production company.

Steve invited Matt to everything we did, even as a family. Matt brought out the best in Steve, and that helped. One night after rehearsals, Steve asked Matt to go with me in the limo to pick up our talent agents from the airport. It was a two-hour drive, and it was the first time I was alone with Matt. At the time, I was in my ninth month of pregnancy, so I had to waddle into the limo. I prayed that God would somehow use our driving time for me to share Jesus with Matt. God answered that prayer, and I got the privilege of praying with him to receive Christ. Steve knows the Bible inside and out and began teaching it to Matt when he traveled with us.

I was sure that meeting Matt was a God thing. He was like a best friend and brother to me, so all my defenses were down. Although he was good-looking, I wasn't attracted to him at the time.

Now let me fast-forward into the "Lifetime movie" part of the story. This man became like family to us. He attended all our son's birthday parties and significant family events. Steve and I both loved him very much. Even though I would normally caution a married couple not to have a single, good-looking man or woman hang out too much with them on a regular basis, because it was under the mask of ministry, it somehow happened to us. I didn't think there was even a chance that I could fall for anybody while I was married—not because my marriage wasn't horrible but because I loved God with all my heart. I felt there was no way I was going to divorce, no matter how miserable I was.

I went so many years without love that I earned my "doctorate degree in denial" and convinced myself that I had no needs as long as I was meeting the needs of others. Although I never had the love of my husband, I didn't realize how empty I actually was. I thought I had mastered surviving a loveless marriage, but anniversaries that were never celebrated were the hardest, and birthday dates that never happened made me feel like I was unworthy of love.

One night, I begged God for a breakthrough. I went to Steve with desperate tears in my eyes and said, "I need you to dial in to me. I need you to love me well so I don't feel so alone. I feel like you're leaving me wide open to fall."

I'll never forget his response.

He said, "Sheri Rose, it's not up to me to make you feel loved. It's up to God."

Desperately, I screamed, "If that's Jesus's job, then why did I marry you? God's Word says you're supposed to love me like He does, and I don't feel loved at all!"

Steve was so frustrated with me, he slammed our bedroom door and walked out. Needless to say, we had a very empty and exasperated marriage. My hope and my heart for my husband died that day. That was all the devil needed. It gave him an open door to deliver someone else to love me.

I never really thought I would walk through that demonic door because I had already seen what it did to my parents and our family. I knew the road of infidelity leads to destruction. But Scripture says, "Do not think you are standing strong or you too will fall."

Right after that fight, I found out I was pregnant and miscarried a baby. I fell into a deep pit of despair and no longer wanted to produce showcases. We came off the road, and Steve had to get a job. He was very angry at me once the traveling ended. We were home together more than we ever had been, and I realized how bad my marriage really was. My husband and I separated seven times throughout our marriage.

During one of those periods of separation, I went to San Diego for a convention. Matt still lived there, so I asked if he could give me a ride to the convention (about an hour and a half drive from the airport). He said he'd be happy to pick me up.

On the way to the convention, Matt looked at me and said, "I want to marry someone just like you. Can you find me a wife?" With that, of course, the Jewish matchmaker in me went right to work! I happened to meet a wonderful Christian girl at the very convention where I was speaking. That night, I set them up for their first date. Six months later, they were engaged to be married. Matt's fiancée, Ann, asked if I would be her matron of honor because she wanted to honor me for setting them up. Ironically, during the weekend of the wedding, I was hospitalized for food poisoning and couldn't attend. I know now why God kept me from being in those wedding photos.

Let me fast-forward again. Matt and Ann had been married for two years, and Steve and I were still struggling through our marriage with several on-and-off periods of separation. We lived in Arizona but visited Southern California often to see my dad and to have double dates with Matt and Ann.

One night, Steve and I had one of our worst fights ever, and I knew we were in trouble. I was drowning in hopelessness and starving for love. I decided to fly to San Diego to see my dad again, but I wanted to go alone. Once again, Matt picked me up from the airport and drove me to my dad's house. We stayed there for several hours and hung out while I cried my eyes out about my marriage. Matt was so kind. He listened and offered comfort. Because I had never felt comfort from my own husband, the comfort of a man felt healing. The enemy knew how desperate I was, and he's no fool. He saw a perfect opportunity for me to fall in a moment of weakness.

At one point, Matt looked at me with tears in his eyes and said, "I'm just so sorry, Sheri Rose. I'm heartbroken that you're not loved well because for years I have watched you love others so well." Matt's heart was so similar to mine. We both were very compassionate and had hearts full of mercy for humanity.

Those few hours together crying and being vulnerable started a period of time where I began to get to know Matt more as a friend. Over time, I came to realize that we were exactly alike in just about every way, even in how we processed our thoughts. I began to realize he was everything I had ever wanted in a man. Of course, I knew I could never tell him that—he was married, and I was fighting for my own marriage. However, that seed was planted by Satan, and my mind became consumed with Matt. I went back to Arizona, but we talked every day on the phone for hours. We started to call each other best friends. By this time, I had become a Christian speaker and was traveling regularly to share the love of Christ with others. Matt and I became so close that he was the only one I wanted to pray with before I spoke. It seemed very innocent because we never put words to our feelings. Then we started praying together every day, and I convinced myself that maybe this was actually a gift from God. Looking back, I know it wasn't. God never gifts you someone else's husband.

The reality was, it was a set-up by Satan. These phone calls, prayers, and long talks went on for about six months. We never saw each other face-to-face; thank God we lived in different states. He was still in California, and I was in Arizona, so you can imagine the fantasy that we built up in our minds even though neither of us ever talked about it. I truly believe that if it wasn't for our individual love for God, the story would have played out very differently than it did.

Around this time, I went to visit my mentors in Northern California to let them know I was falling in love with a married man whom I had led to the Lord and set up with his wife. What a soap opera I had entered! I knew I needed them to help me get out before it went to the next level. They showed convicting compassion as their tears fell for me. They held me as I cried out in desperation to both of them.

Scott, my mentor dad, said, "Sheri Rose, you deserve love, and I am so sorry you walked into the first trap by ignoring our warnings and your father's not to marry Steve. But we're not going to let you fall into the second trap that Satan has set to destroy you and the ministry He has given you." As they held me, he continued, "I want to share a story of how Eskimos trap and kill wolves."

In that vulnerable moment, all I could think was, *Are you kidding me? I'm fighting to be free from an emotional affair and he wants to tell me a story about Eskimos and wolves?* I asked God to give me eyes to see what He wanted me to see in this story.

Scott began to share, "Eskimos have a very interesting method of luring in wolves when they need to kill one for food and their warm fur. You see, Sheri Rose, what the Eskimos do when they need to kill a wolf is make a 'bloodsicle' of sorts. It's like a popsicle of frozen blood. They start by taking a very sharp knife and dipping it into blood. With one coat of blood, they set it in the cold and let that freeze. This process is repeated until there's enough blood frozen on the knife to cover it completely. Once the bloodsicle is complete, it's laid on the ice in front of their igloo. The wolf is aware but still cautiously approaches the bloodsicle. Though the wolf is wary, he begins to lick the blood anyway. The wolf is wise enough to see the danger but he is convinced that he can enjoy just enough and then stop before he gets to the knife. The problem is, once he starts licking the blood, he can't stop, and pretty soon he licks straight to the knife. Before he knows it, the wolf cuts through his own tongue and slowly bleeds to death."

"That's a really great story, but I'm not tempted by Matt. I have never even kissed him." I broke out hysterically crying. "What I mean is, I am not just tempted by him, I'm completely in love with him...so much so that I know how dangerous of a situation I'm in."

I realized in that moment that I was the wolf.

They warned me again, saying, "Sheri Rose, it won't be easy to cut this off...but if you don't, it will kill everything inside you. Your future will be changed forever if you don't run away from this."

I told them I needed their help and for God to fill my heart with His love for me, or the ripple effects could be devastating. "I would rather be in pain myself the rest of my life than take him for myself and destroy so much," I said. "I know I need to end everything now."

They compassionately said, "We are going to fast and pray until this thing is done."

The next day, they took me to the airport where I was flying out for an event I was speaking at in Palm Springs, California. I was processing so many different emotions on that flight. I was angry at my husband for not showing me love. I was mad at myself for falling into this trap. I was hurting because I felt like I would never be loved well by a man.

Suddenly, the pilot came over the loudspeaker to announce, "I'm sorry to tell you, but we've been warned there is a strong wind shear, and we cannot land in Palm Springs. I'm going to defer us to San Diego, where you can stay the night, and we can try again in the morning."

In that moment, my heart sank. All I could think was, *God, are you kidding me? I'm trying to be obedient and get away from Matt, and You're taking me to the very city he lives in! Why would*

You take me there when I'm trying to do the right thing? But God clearly had a bigger picture and knew exactly what I needed to be able to break free.

As soon as I landed, I called my dad, who lived in San Diego, to let him know I needed to stay with him because my flight had been grounded in San Diego. To my surprise, he responded, "I can't pick you up and you can't stay at my house. I'm in New York, and my alarms are set. But I will get you a ride and a place to stay." Then he hung up. Five minutes later, he called me back and said, "Rosie, I have you all set. I got a hold of Matt. He and his wife are coming to get you, and you can stay at their house tonight. It's the best I could do. There's a big convention in town and hotels are booked solid this weekend."

I was mortified. My dad had no idea I had just decided to break off my friendship with Matt. My head was spinning, my heart was freaking out, and I couldn't understand what God was doing.

My dad had told Matt to meet me in the baggage claim area at the airport. I'll never forget going down that escalator and seeing Matt with his wife...to my shock, she was very pregnant. During our endless phone affair, Matt had never told me they were going to have a baby. Honestly, that was the sobering I needed. I felt physically sick in my soul. I knew that I had not done anything physical with her husband. I hadn't even put words to my feelings. But I also knew in my heart that I was in love with him, and he was now going to be a father.

Ann greeted me with a hug and asked if I would spend the weekend with her and Matt since my dad was out of town. She knew I had flown into California to speak at a Christian women's conference, and she asked if she could go with me. There was a knot in my belly as big as the baby in hers. Everything in me screamed, *God, please don't make me stay at their home!*

Looking back, I can see how God had set this up to free me from Matt forever. When He sees us temped by something that could kill us, He will do whatever He can to help if we ask Him to. He will always rescue His beloved children from the devil! God went to such extremes to help me get out that you may wonder if this story could really happen. I promise it did, though sometimes I still can't believe it myself.

As I walked into their home for the first time, my eyes were opened even more to the depth of my love for Matt. My greatest nightmare became a reality as I realized that if I didn't get out of there, I would become "the other woman"—the one I never wanted to be. This nightmare had haunted me through my own childhood with my mom, so how could I even be tempted to do the same?

Overwhelmed with emotion, I decided I had to get out of that house and go for a run. Matt stopped me, saying, "It's dark, and it's not safe for a woman to run alone out there." But I promised to run in the brightly lit baseball field.

As soon as I got to there, I threw myself on the wet grass. I put my head on the ground and screamed out loud, "God, get me out of this, please! I love this man so much. You have to take this love away and help me walk away!" While I was still face-down with my headphones on and my music turned up to a volume I hoped would drown out my painful thoughts, I saw a shadow behind me.

Deep down, I knew it was Matt, and I realized he had just heard me confess my feelings of love for him for the first time.

I stood up slowly and turned around to see tears streaming down his face as he asked, "Why didn't you tell me you were in love with me? I have always been in love with you."

He tried to hug me, but I backed away. "Don't touch me. This can never happen. We have to get out of this...we have to untangle this." I begged him to go back to the house. I reassured him that I would join him and Ann later once God helped me pull myself together.

My heart was shattered at that moment because honestly, I had never really been in love until I'd gotten to know Matt, and he had just declared his love for me. I'd never met a man who made me come alive inside like he did, and in my humanity, I wanted him for myself. I begged God to give me the strength to walk away from what I wanted in exchange for His will.

To be honest, I could not imagine what life would feel like not talking to Matt every day. He had been in our lives for over nine years, and in the previous seven months, he'd become like oxygen to help me breathe through a really bad marriage. I so wished I could run away at that very moment, but God knew there was more.

All of a sudden, the park lights went out, and I was in pitch darkness in the park, which was exactly how my heart felt in that very moment. My body felt numb, and the grief had a gravity that pulled me down to the ground. I wanted to die that night. But as I lay there on the wet ground in the darkness, I heard a voice whisper in my spirit, *Sheri Rose, I know you've lost your direction, but you must get up and just do the next right thing.*

I knew it was the voice of my Heavenly Father, and I knew He would help no matter how heartbroken I felt. I knew I couldn't trust my feelings and that I needed the Holy Spirit more than I ever had before to give me exactly what I needed to walk away. I knew I could not look too far ahead. That would be too much for me to take. I decided I would take one breath at a time and trust God to help me do the next right thing.

That dark night, I gave my heart back to God and let Him love me back to life. I stood up and stumbled my way back to Matt and Ann's house. When I walked in the door, I felt different. My heart began to break—not for myself, but for Ann. I knew God had rearranged my heart. My love for my God triumphed over my love for Matt. We all said an awkward goodnight.

I couldn't sleep that night. I cried for hours on end. The next morning, I had to push past my feelings to get ready to speak at the women's event. All I could think was, *How am I going to survive the drive with Ann and also find the courage to get up and speak to these women in the midst of fighting all of these feelings?*

Just then, Ann came into the kitchen. She made me breakfast and then got ready to go with me to the conference. As a surprise gift, my always-doting dad had sent a limo to drive us to the event in Palm Springs. Daddy still had no idea what had transpired. When the limo arrived, Matt helped us load up and prayed over our time together. We sat in the back of the beautiful limo filled with fresh fruit, flowers, and sparkling water. We were sitting on opposite sides of the car, eight feet apart. Ann and I are total talkers, but this time, there was a very scary silence between us.

I could feel Ann staring at me, but I could not look at her. I am never like this—I usually love to connect with whomever I'm with.

But Satan's trap always keeps us bound up from being ourselves. Several minutes into our silent drive, Ann got up, crawled across the limo, and sat next to me. She looked me square in the eye and asked, "Sheri Rose, are you in love with my husband?"

I felt sick. I knew it was going to hurt, but I had to be honest. It was clear that God had provided this moment of truth to stop that devastating scenario from becoming a reality.

"Yes, but I am never going to act on it," I said, "and nothing ever happened physically."

My heart was torn open for her. All I could think about was how she must have felt in that moment, stuck in a limo with me. I hated myself, and I couldn't help but wonder over and over how I ever could have let this happen. I had been the trusted friend who set Ann up with her husband. We cried together about the unspoken affair of the heart as it was now a reality we both had to deal with.

I asked her, "What can I do? I promise, I will do anything to undo this and fix it."

At that moment, the limo broke down right in the middle of the desert—*another God thing.* I never got to that event in Palm Springs because God knew there was no way I could have pushed through that painful moment to go and speak! Never in my life have I been so grateful to be stuck in a desert, yet there I was with Ann. We were both uncomfortable—in every way possible. It was over 100 degrees, and the limo had no air-conditioning since it was broken down. Once again, I was waiting for Matt to come pick us up. The waiting seemed like an eternity of uncertainty.

Matt finally arrived. He had no idea about the conversation that had transpired between me and Ann. She asked me not to tell him until she'd had a chance to talk to him alone. I honored her request. You can imagine the "silent suffering" in the car as Matt, Ann, and I all drove back to their home together so I could get my luggage.

Matt kept staring at me in the rearview mirror, trying to get a read on what I was feeling. He reached over to hold Ann's hand, but she pulled away. There we were, three shattered hearts in one awkwardly silent car. I knew that only God could piece any of our broken lives back together. When we pulled into their driveway, I immediately got out of the car so they would have time to talk alone, went inside to pack my luggage, and called a friend to pick me up. My soul felt sick. I couldn't see how I could ever get through this.

As I was leaving, Matt chased after me. I begged him to save his family. I told him I had promised both his wife and God that I would never connect with him again.

I was so traumatized by this experience that I tried to cancel all my speaking events after that day. I told each church what had happened and why I wanted to cancel. For whatever reason, God did not make a way for me to get out of one event; none of them would cancel my contracts. One pastor's wife stopped me in my explanation, saying, "Sheri Rose, you didn't have an affair. You walked away." Another said they had prayed about releasing me, and God showed them if they let me cancel, I might never want to speak again. They were probably right—I would've never moved beyond the shame. I would have been chained to a moment in time and stopped doing what God had called me to do: share His love with others.

It took years for me to heal from this affair of the heart. I knew God had forgiven me, and I knew I did the right thing by walking away, but I could not get past the pain of what had happened.

What Can God Do?

One day, a country pastor and his wife invited me to sit on their porch for lunch with them after a speaking engagement in Texas. They said they had something to share with me that could set me free. They asked me to tell the story of my parents' affair. As I told how I was conceived in adultery, the pastor stopped me, interjecting, "Sheri Rose, forgive yourself! You did not fail! In fact, you broke the curse of adultery over your family by walking away from what you wanted."

Then the pastor's wife hugged me, saying, "Honey, I know how bad it hurts to walk away from someone you love so much. We're proud of you, and so is God."

Their words were like living water that began to nourish my dying soul. I will always thank God for that Texas pastor and his wife because they broke Satan's stronghold on my heart. In that moment, I began to breathe in God's grace and goodness once again.

As usual, God didn't stop there. He knew I needed deeper healing, and He showed me how personal He really is! The following week, I was in Hawaii, speaking at another women's retreat. Afterward, I was sitting on a rock overlooking the ocean, reflecting on the talk I'd had on the porch of the pastor's home in Texas. While

I sat there, my phone buzzed; it was an invitation to speak on a conference tour with Chris Tomlin and Casting Crowns. They offered me eighteen dates. Believe me, I love encouraging and ministering to God's people, but I needed to be freed from this personal pain once and for all. I cried out to God in tears and terror and said, "God, the only way I will do this tour is if You find a way to show me that Matt and Ann's marriage was saved after I walked away."

Because I had kept my promise to never connect with him again, I had no idea what the outcome was. But I needed to know in order to move forward. I had to know they were still together and that everything was OK. I had to know I had not destroyed a family.

Believe it or not, ten minutes after that cry to God, I received a group text from my best friend letting us know that one of our mutual friends had passed away suddenly that day. There were seven of us on that group text, and one of those people was Matt.

My friend reminded us to love our families and cherish the time we have together, and added a picture of her family. This led to a chain reaction of everyone else on the text posting pictures of theirs. Then it happened: Matt posted a picture with him, Ann, *and their two sons* from a family vacation they had taken to Hawaii.

Then God got even crazier. I zoomed in on Matt's picture to realize that not only been had it been taken at the same resort I was staying at, but they had been sitting on the very rock I was sitting on at that moment, just six months earlier.

Not only did God answer my prayer for healing by sending a pastor to show me how I had broken the curse of adultery over my own family, but He also answered my prayer of reassurance that Matt and Ann's family was intact minutes after I had cried out to Him. It was over the top for me to see how personal our God is!

The redemption of the story was not God's sending another man to love me but in the legacy. He used my worst mistake to reverse the curse of adultery over my own children's futures. Ultimately, a family was saved, and two boys still have their father.

What Can I Do?

Get Away from Temptation

God loves you so much, and He wants what's best for you. He will do anything to provide a way for you to escape temptation. If you feel yourself falling in love with a married man, your pastor, or any man who is not yours, I encourage you to walk away. Do whatever it takes: get a different job, get a different church, whatever you need. There is nothing better than knowing you did what was right in God's sight. No temporary pleasure is better than God's promises for you. Walk away now, and don't forfeit the plans God has for you. If you have a friend who is about to fall in love with a married man, warn her—do whatever you can to help her get out before it's too late. Remember, when you walk away, you're saving another family from falling apart.

Get Accountability

"If you think you are standing strong, be careful not to fall." (1 Corinthians 10:12)

I think many times we put our confidence in our own strength or let our wants override wisdom from the Word. Wisdom and godly counsel will always give us the option of peace and prevent poor decisions. Wisdom is the only way to build a solid foundation that Satan cannot crumble. Keep in mind that you can't control other people's decisions, but you can control your reactions. I thought I was strong. I never thought I would fall, so I never thought I needed accountability. But no matter how much you love Jesus and no matter how good your intentions are, you're still human—you need accountability, and so do I. This life was not meant to be done alone. Get yourself in a small group and be transparent. Find a girlfriend you can be totally real with in any weakness. Let her be real with you and help you do what's right. The Bible says, "As iron sharpens iron, so one man sharpens another." Be with people who will sharpen you, who will make you better, who will call you up. But make sure that your accountability partner isn't just a critic. They have to care for you and be kind to you as well.

Get Back Up

God's Word teaches us, "The godly may trip seven times, but they will get up again" (Proverbs 24:16).

Notice the scripture says even a righteous man falls. The hardest thing for me was to get back up afterwards. I didn't feel like I deserved God's grace. Then I remembered the Bible's heroes and how all of them did something that would disqualify them from doing God's work and living His will if they'd stopped after their sin. Keep in mind that there is not a soul on this earth who won't experience failure, disappointment, and discouragement. Our beloved King David had to get up from the shame of neglecting his duty and committing adultery. The Apostle Peter had to get up from the guilt of denying Jesus three times after bragging that he loved the Lord more than everyone else. Do not misunderstand me—there is a price to pay when we fall and sin against God. However, the same God who disciplines us because He loves us also sent us a Savior to give us the power to get back up and fight on.

Be Obedient at Any Cost

To be honest, I've never loved anybody more in my life than Matt. I never knew it was even possible to have that kind of love for a man. Walking away from him was the hardest thing I ever did, and it took years to heal from the heartache of missing him. But the price was too big to pay to spend the rest of my life with someone else's husband or to take a father from his kids. God has been good to me, and He's giving me back something better than a man: He blessed my obedience with a legacy of faith that will live on long after I'm gone.

Today, I have peace in my heart and the joy of walking with Jesus in the purpose He created me for. Now that I'm older and looking back on this story that happened over twenty-five years ago, I can testify that the peace of God and the joy of repairing the damage done trump any temporary pleasure of this life. I've learned that the redemption isn't in a better man to love me, but in a better life in Christ!

HIS LOVE LETTER TO YOU

My Beloved Daughter,

I want to do more for you than keep you from evil. I want to free your heart from the desire to sin. When you are tempted, take authority over evil and speak My words of deliverance out loud—you will discover that My power is greater than the enemies of your soul. I am your power, your safety. I can keep you on the road to everlasting life and will let nothing destroy My perfect will for you. I have set you apart for a purpose far greater than any pleasure this world has to offer. So call to Me before you stumble into a trap, and I will make a way of escape. Seek Me, and I will give you the power to prevail. The more you taste My goodness, the less you will crave any temporary temptation. I am strong in your every weakness, and I will give you strength to walk through or away from any situation. Now get up and go in My name, and let Me help you live a balanced life!

Love,

Your King and your Keeper

"And God is faithful. He will not allow the temptation to be more than you can stand. When you are tempted, he will show you a way out so that you can endure." (1 Corinthians 10:13)

Chapter 8

BEYOND FATHERLESSNESS

GOD, HEAL ME THROUGH THIS ABANDONMENT AND HELP ME KNOW YOU AS MY HEAVENLY FATHER.

Rochelle was raised by an alcoholic single mom who did not believe in God. When she would ask about her dad, her mom would shut her down by saying, "It doesn't matter. As far as I'm concerned, your father doesn't exist, and neither does God."

Even though Rochelle had a bad home life, she was a good girl who made good choices. It was a miracle she had such a good head on her shoulders under the circumstances. She was the head cheerleader, but her mom never went to any of her games—even the last one, when she was crowned homecoming queen. Rochelle was on the honor roll all four years of high school and won a scholarship to the college of her choice—but at the awards ceremony, there was no father waiting with roses and no mother there to say, "I'm proud of you, honey."

On Rochelle's eigthteenth birthday, she begged her mom to tell her who her birth dad was so she could find him. As usual, her mom refused—then served herself another drink. Rochelle had never berated her mom, but after eighteen years, she'd had enough. "Mom, I deserve to know who my real father is! Please tell me his name and where I can find him!" she yelled.

In a bitter, remorseful tone, her mom said, "Sit down, Rochelle. Listen, I am so ashamed to tell you this, but on my eighteenth birthday, I got stupidly drunk, had sex with some guy I didn't know, and got pregnant with you. I never saw him again, and the truth is I didn't even know his name." Rochelle hung on her every word because her mom had never shared anything personal about herself until that day. "Listen, Rochelle, I know I haven't been the best mom in the world. But at least I'm doing better than my parents. They abandoned me when I was six. I haven't seen them since. That's why you've never met them." She paused for a minute, then stammered, "I am sorry I'm not better at this."

Rochelle began to cry tears of compassion for her mom and herself. In that moment, she felt like half of her would always be missing because she would never know who her biological daddy was.

Rochelle had always been the strong one in the family. But for the first time, her mom was moved by Rochelle's pain. She walked over, held her daughter, and cried with her. Rochelle felt like she finally had a mom, even if it was only for a night.

The next day, Rochelle asked her best friend, Lindsay, "What does it feel like to have a father who loves and adores you?"

Lindsay's heart broke for Rochelle. She quickly prayed, "God, give me the words." Then she lovingly said, "Rochelle, actually you do have a real father—it is your Heavenly Father. He loves you very much and wants to be close to you."

Rochelle had no idea how to respond. Lindsay had been a Christian for a long time, but because she knew that Rochelle came from an atheistic family, she had never discussed faith with her before. But God had opened a door in Rochelle's heart to know Him, and Lindsay seized the moment. She asked if Rochelle wanted to go with her to youth group that night. Rochelle excitedly said yes!

The girls walked in a little late; the youth pastor was talking about how much our Heavenly Father loves His children. Then he talked about being adopted into God's royal family when you receive Jesus as your savior.

Lindsay was so happy that her youth pastor was sharing the same love of God that she had with Rochelle. She could see from the tears rolling down Rochelle's cheeks that God's presence was touching her. As the service ended, the youth band began to play softly, and the lights went dim so the kids could reflect as the pastor led them in a salvation prayer. Rochelle bowed her head, and her tears continued as she repeated it with passion in every word. Then she felt something she had never experienced before: it felt as though an invisible Father's arms were holding her. Her heart finally began to heal that night as she discovered that she wasn't fatherless; she was a daughter of the King!

She could now see that even though her earthly father had never been in her life, her Heavenly Father had been there for everything from the time she was born. Rochelle's tears turned to joy as she knew she'd gotten her heart's deepest desire—she'd met her *real Father,* and His name was God. Once Rochelle gave her life to Jesus, she wanted to learn everything about her Heavenly Father and the royal family she was now a part of. She read the Bible for hours that summer. Rochelle would often say with a twinkle in her eyes, "I can't wait to see how my Heavenly Father is going to write my life story. After all, the Bible says He is the author of my life."

She attended every church and community outreach event so she could serve others. She told everybody about her Heavenly Father and how they could receive Jesus as their savior and become part of His royal family too. The only person Rochelle kept her faith from was her mom. She wanted badly to tell her mom about Jesus, but she feared her rejection. They were just beginning to have a relationship. But Rochelle continued to pray for her mom's heart and for the courage to share about Jesus before she left for college.

One Sunday, she found out a world-renowned choir was coming to their church. Twenty college-aged kids from all over the world would sing and share their testimonies. Rochelle knew she had to go, so Lindsay picked her up that evening, and they went together. When Rochelle hopped in the car, she joyfully exclaimed, "Lindsay, I just know something special is going to happen tonight!"

The church was decorated absolutely beautifully in honor of the guest choir. The small sanctuary had sparkling lights everywhere. Lindsay and Rochelle sat in the front row so they wouldn't miss a thing. When the choir began to sing, their voices harmonized so perfectly that it was like the sound of Heaven from every country praising our Jesus in one accord. Between each life-altering song, individual members of the choir came forward to share about the tests and trials God had used to prepare them for their purposes.

Rochelle loved God stories, but after hearing some of their testimonies, she felt conflicted. Part of her couldn't wait to have her own faith adventures, but the other part of her feared what she might face if she stepped into ministry. But more than anything, she wanted to make her Heavenly Father proud and do something to make a difference in His world.

The fear stopped, and so did her heart, when a very handsome young man from Puerto Rico named Ricardo stepped up to the podium. As he began to speak, Rochelle's heart melted. He talked about his passion for following God and how God had led his grandma to start an orphanage in his homeland. Ricardo had spent time at the orphanage since he was a little boy and spoke lovingly about the children there and how, though they didn't have an earthly family, they'd become part of God's family.

Rochelle felt God using his every word to speak directly to her heart. She had always had a strange curiosity about Puerto Rico, and hearing about the land and the people only sparked that curiosity more. Hearing about orphaned children who knew they had a family with God spoke right to the piece of her heart that still ached. Every fear in her soul left. Then Ricardo closed with this truth: "The safest place to be in the whole world is wherever God sends you."

Rochelle felt God depositing a deep love in her heart for Ricardo. Yes, he was a tall, dark, handsome Puerto Rican with a cool accent any girl would be attracted to. But she knew it was more than a crush. This felt like God was calling her to be by his side. Rochelle leaned over to her friend with her eyes still on Ricardo and whispered, "Not only is he gorgeous, he's godly too. I'm going to marry that man!"

Lindsay tried her best to contain her laughter, but she loved her friend's audacity. "Yeah, right, Rochelle. You know every girl in this room is thinking the same thing. Should I send out the wedding invitations before you meet him or wait for your first date?"

Rochelle laughed. "Absolutely send them now!"

After the service, several girls bolted to gather around Ricardo. Rochelle felt a moment of panic as she thought, *How in the world am I ever going to get his attention and make a connection before I leave?*

Just then, Rochelle remembered that the choir had handed out cards that evening as people came in, inviting them to write their prayer requests on the cards and hand them to a choir member at the end of the night. *I am definitely in need of some prayer if I want to secure my place as Ricardo's wife, especially with all these girls around him*, Rochelle thought, giggling to herself. She grabbed her card, and with one deep breath, said a quick prayer and got in line with all the other girls. She tried to think about what she would say, but when she finally got face-to-face with Ricardo, she found herself speechless. So she just handed him the card.

Ricardo glanced at it and said, "Hey, your card is empty."

"Yes, I know," she said with a smile. "Why don't you fill it out, and I can pray for *you* this year instead." From the look on his face, she could see she had touched his heart. He began writing on the card. "Feel free to write as many prayer requests as you want. There's no limit, other than the size of the card," Rochelle said.

Ricardo finished writing, handed her the card, and thanked her for praying for him. Then he turned his attention to the next girl waiting in line.

As they walked out, Lindsay could tell her friend was discouraged. Rochelle lamented that she hadn't gotten the connection she had hoped for. But when they got in the car, Rochelle looked at the card. Both her face and her faith lit up as she read what Ricardo had written:

"Pray that God makes a way for me to see you again."

The two girls screamed with excitement.

"This is going to have to be a God thing for this to happen—we didn't get each other's phone numbers, we don't have any mutual friends, and we live in different countries," Rochelle said.

"Where is your faith, girl? Let's pray now!" Lindsay said.

That night when she got home, Rochelle put the prayer card under her pillow and picked up her Bible. She was excited to ask God for the miracle that Ricardo had asked for on his card. In some ways, it felt like she was praying a jigsaw-puzzle prayer with a lot of the pieces missing. She opened her Bible to Matthew 19, where she'd left off that morning. She felt God whisper the words written on the page as she read Matthew 19:26: "Humanly speaking, it is impossible. But with God everything is possible." That night, she prayed more as she drifted off to sleep. She felt peace knowing she could trust her Heavenly Daddy to take care of every detail of her future.

The end of summer came, and it was time for Rochelle to go to college. Before she left, she knew she needed to share Christ's love with her mom. She prayed hard for the right words, and then walked into her mom's room and sat by her on her bed. She hesitantly began to share that she'd found God and that He'd become her Heavenly Father. Then she asked her mom if she wanted to pray to receive Christ.

Her mom freaked out and screamed adamantly, "God doesn't exist!" She was so angry that she kicked Rochelle out of the house that night. Rochelle worked all alone to load every earthly possession she had into her car. She left her house without so much as a "goodbye" from her mom. She drove to Lindsay's house in tears, completely crushed and confused. Not only was her relationship with her mom now over, but her mom had refused a relationship with God.

Lindsay's mom greeted her at the door with a hug and sat her down to talk. Rochelle had questions she needed a mom to answer. Still crying, Rochelle asked, "Did I say something wrong about God to my mom? Why didn't God answer my prayer for my mom to know Him? Wouldn't God want that?"

Lindsay's mom lovingly replied, "Honey, God doesn't puppet people. They have to choose to love Him and let Him love them back."

Lindsay came downstairs to comfort her friend. She reassured Rochelle that her Heavenly Father was proud of her for sharing His love with her mom, even it if wasn't well received. Rochelle was so grateful for Lindsay and her family. Their house had become her second home.

Rochelle spent the night, planning on driving to college the next day. But she couldn't sleep. As crazy as it sounds, she felt like God was leading her to change colleges at the last minute. She loved both colleges and had really struggled to choose. The college she chose kept her close to her Lindsay and church. If she went to the other college, she would have to move to Texas. She really needed confirmation from God and a miracle to make the switch.

The next morning, Rochelle called the school in Texas, and God confirmed what Rochelle was feeling. The school welcomed her with open arms and made every necessary arrangement for her to move to Texas, including a dorm to live in. When she arrived, some of the girls came to meet her. She felt right at home; instantly, she knew she had made the right choice.

But what she didn't expect was who she would see when she walked into college orientation: Ricardo was sitting in the auditorium, and the seat next to him was open.

Rochelle tried her best to remain calm as she ran over and slipped into it. She knew if she wasn't quick, another girl would take the spot she had prayed about all summer.

Ricardo was distracted, talking to a buddy on his other side. Rochelle anxiously waited to see if he would remember her and what he had written on that prayer card. More importantly, she wondered if he would be excited that God had answered his prayer.

When Ricardo stood up to stretch, he was awestruck to find Rochelle sitting right next to him. His smile was huge as he looked at her with complete astonishment. "I can't believe it! You're here! God actually answered my prayer!"

He pulled Rochelle out of her chair and hugged her in front of everybody. Rochelle realized she had heard her Heavenly Father's voice, and she was so glad she had listened.

During orientation, the school's director of missions shared about upcoming events for the year, including several mission trips. One particular trip caught Rochelle's attention: it would take place the following summer in Puerto Rico. Rochelle had always felt drawn to the island. Plus, she thought it would be an amazing thing to do with Ricardo—maybe she'd even get to meet his family! She knew they didn't know each other well enough for her to say anything, so she waited on God's timing. He'd already put together the missing pieces for her and Ricardo to meet, so surely a little mission trip would be nothing if He wanted it to happen.

Over the next three months, Rochelle and Ricardo became best friends. They were together all the time. One day while they were at lunch, she saw the paperwork for the Puerto Rico trip in the college cafeteria and picked it up as they moved through the lunch line. When they sat down, she looked in his eyes with a great big smile and said, "I think we should to do this together!"

He looked into her sweet face and said, "How can I resist?"

Summer was upon them in no time, and so was the trip. It lasted the entire summer, and Rochelle loved every minute of it. The last stop was in Ricardo's hometown. On the bus headed there, she held his hand, looked into his eyes, and said, "I'm so excited to meet your family today!"

He got uncomfortably quiet, which was very unlike him. Rochelle asked, "Ricardo, are you OK? Did I say something wrong?"

He hesitated for a moment, then replied, "Rochelle, I'm nervous. I've never brought a girl home before, because, well ... I've never been in love before. So I guess I'm just a little nervous to bring you to meet my parents, and I'm a little nervous about how they're going to feel about meeting you. My mom will know right away I'm in love with you. I hope she falls head over heels with you like I did. I just wish my grandma was here to meet you too."

Part of her wanted to jump into his arms with excitement because he'd just said he was in love with her; he'd never said that before. But the other part feared another mother's rejection. Love trumped her fear, so she jumped into his lap, wrapped her arms around him, and asked, "What? You're in love with me?"

Ricardo laughed and replied, "How can you not see that I'm in love with you? I spend every waking moment with you." Then he squeezed her, and they gazed out the window as Ricardo pointed out various details of his quaint little hometown.

When the bus parked, Ricardo grabbed Rochelle's hand and led her through some narrow neighborhood streets to a small house. The moment was upon them, and Ricardo was ready to face his fears and let his parents meet the woman he loved.

When Rochelle and Ricardo walked into his parents' house, she felt so welcomed—what a relief! Rochelle spoke very little Spanish, and Ricardo's mom and dad didn't speak any English at all. But the language barrier didn't block the kindness and love they were showing her. Even though she couldn't understand much of what they were saying, she could see the look of love in his parents' eyes.

Ricardo's mom had prepared a feast for them and asked them all to gather around the table as a family. Rochelle had never done that before. Her own mom had never even made a meal for her.

This was a precious moment, and she realized how badly she wanted to be part of a family. At that moment, she felt like God was giving her one through Ricardo and his parents.

Ricardo's mom kept staring at her son and Rochelle together at the table. He could tell she not only approved of Rochelle, but adored her. He was ecstatic. His parents saw something in Rochelle that brought out the best in their son. When it was time to leave, Ricardo's mom hugged him and whispered something in his ear. He smiled and hugged her tightly as he said goodbye. Then his mom put her hands on Rochelle's face, lovingly looked into her eyes, and said something in a very tender tone. Rochelle could not understand her words, but her heart could interpret his mom's love for her. She knew it was something she had wanted all her life.

As soon as they got out the door, Rochelle asked Ricardo, "What did your mom whisper to you right before we left?"

"She told me that you're the girl she has prayed for since I was a baby," he said, "and if I didn't marry you, I would be missing God's best for me." Then he pulled her toward him and kissed her passionately for the very first time. (And yes, it was as good as she'd imagined it would be.)

A few minutes later, Rochelle pulled back and said, "Please interpret what your mom said to me."

"She told you to take care of her son and love me well."

Rochelle kissed both of Ricardo's cheeks and said, "I would love to take care of you for the rest of your life!"

Rochelle's mission was accomplished on that trip. She got the man, she got his parents' blessing, and she got her Heavenly Father's confirmation! The following months, the couple fell so in love that they couldn't imagine life without each other. Ricardo couldn't wait any longer. He told Rochelle to meet him at their favorite park because he had a surprise for her.

Rochelle got dolled up for him. His heart stopped as she walked up in a blue dress that matched her beautiful blue eyes. The look of love on his face radiated. He kissed her hand, and sat her down at a communion table he had set for them. Then he handed her a beautiful purple velvet box. When she opened it, she saw a uniquely designed antique wedding ring, one like she had never seen before. "Where did you find a ring like this? I adore it! It's so divinely different!"

"It was my grandmother's wedding ring," Ricardo said, his eyes welling up with tears. "She gave it to me the day before she passed away, when I was only thirteen. On that day, she prayed with me for my future bride and told me this ring was for her."

Ricardo got down on one knee and continued, "Rochelle, you are everything I have ever dreamed of in a woman, inside and out. I never actually thought it was possible for my dream to become reality until I met you. I know God made us for each other, and I can't imagine my life without you. Will you marry me?"

Rochelle's heart melted completely. "Your future bride says yes!"

They served each other communion and dedicated their love and their lives to the Lord. Then Ricardo pulled her up with him, and held her close as he began singing her favorite songs.

"Keep singing. I never want you to stop!" she said as she squeezed him tightly, pressing her head into his chest. They danced in the park, and he kept singing in her ear until the sun went down and the security guard kicked them out. That night, as Rochelle slipped into her bed, she realized that not only did she have a Heavenly Father who loved her, but she also now had a mom and a grandma who had prayed for her before they even knew her name.

Rochelle and Ricardo didn't want to wait to start their life together. They got married right away and finished their last two years of college as a married couple. They had two wedding ceremonies—one in Puerto Rico and one in Texas—so that all their spiritual family and college friends could attend. Rochelle loved it because she got to wear her beautiful wedding dress twice!

Sadly, her mom refused to come to either wedding. Ricardo's dad walked her down the aisle of her first wedding, and Lindsay's dad did the same at the wedding in Texas. Lindsay, of course, was her maid of honor.

When they returned from their honeymoon, they were hired as the youth directors of their church. Two years later, their church surprised them with a vacation to celebrate their anniversary and college graduation at the same time. God gave them another surprise gift while they were celebrating—but they didn't get to open it for nine months: it was a beautiful baby girl.

They named her Clarita after the grandma who had given Ricardo the wedding ring that Rochelle proudly wore. They adored their baby girl. Ricardo would always talk about all the things he wanted to do with Clarita as she grew up.

Listening to Ricardo go on about that made Rochelle giggle. "Your Clarita is only a baby, and you're talking about her first day of kindergarten, her prom, and her wedding day!" she'd say sweetly.

They laughed and hugged as Rochelle told Ricardo, "Clarita is the most blessed daughter in the world to have a daddy like you!"

One evening, when Clarita was only three months old, Rochelle and Ricardo took their first date together as new parents. Though they struggled to leave their baby girl for the first time, they also couldn't wait to get in each other's arms and have some time together again. Rochelle once again got dolled up and wore the blue dress she'd worn when Ricardo had proposed to her. It was winter, and Ricardo had gone out to the car to warm it up for her. As she walked toward him, he looked at her like he was seeing her for the first time. She got into the car, kissed him, and they drove off for their dinner date. Ricardo kept looking at Rochelle's beautiful face at each stoplight.

"How do you do that?" she said.

"How do I do what?" he asked.

"How do you look at me like you're falling in love with me all over again?"

"Because every time I look at you, I do fall in love all over again. Honestly, my heart is overwhelmed that I get to spend the rest of my days with you."

Ricardo reached for Rochelle's hand and kissed it tenderly...then looked up to see a big Chevy truck running a red light at sixty miles an hour. There was no time to react. The truck struck Ricardo's side of the car. Immediately, it flew like a spinning top through the street and flipped upside down. All Rochelle remembered was waking up to see Ricardo knocked unconscious; his head was bleeding badly.

The paramedics pulled Ricardo out first. Rochelle could see what was happening but couldn't feel anything but terror. Rochelle's body was hurt badly, but nothing hurt more than her heart in that moment. She heard the sirens on the ambulance rushing the love of her life to the hospital. Rochelle was as flipped out as the upside-down car the paramedics pulled her from before putting her in a second ambulance.

When she arrived at the hospital, Rochelle just wanted to know if her husband was still alive. The nurses reassured her he'd been taken to one of the best brain surgeons in the area and the doctors were doing everything they could to save his life. Ricardo's surgery seemed to take an eternity, and Rochelle hated that she couldn't be near him as she waited. She begged the ER staff to rush her own tests so she could find her husband.

As they cleaned and bandaged her wounds, she couldn't feel anything but the fear of losing her husband. She kept praying, "God, please don't let him die! Please don't let him die! I don't care what the outcome is, God, but please just don't let him die!"

When Rochelle was released to wait outside the operating room, her heart dropped into her stomach as Ricardo's surgeon approached. She could see from the look on his face that it wasn't good news.

"Mrs. Rodriguez, your husband is still alive but non-responsive. We have him on life support, but his brain is swelling and we could not stop the bleeding. We're going to run a few more tests to see if there's anything else we can do. I'm so sorry I don't have better news," he said seriously.

Ricardo's parents flew in from Puerto Rico to help care for Clarita. Weeks turned into months in the hospital. Rochelle was emotionally and physically exhausted. Every day brought more tests, tons of decisions, and so many uncertainties. She battled to believe that her baby girl would have a daddy when everything was done. The last thing she wanted was for Clarita to be fatherless, like she had been. She was heartbroken for herself and for her beloved husband. Would Ricardo be there for his baby girl the way he dreamed he would? Their life as a family had just begun. Was she going to be a single mother?

I'm only twenty-five years old, she thought.

Bad news always seemed to accompany the doctors who visited their room—and the more specialized the doctor, the worse the news. The final blow came one day when Ricardo's brain surgeon said, "Rochelle, we need to have a serious talk about Ricardo's outlook. The terrible truth is he has suffered such extensive back and brain injuries from the car accident that he will never walk again. We have done everything possible for him, and I'm sorry to be the one to tell you that his current state will likely never improve."

Rochelle stared at him blankly as he continued, "Your husband will always be a quadriplegic, living in a mostly vegetative state. He will never be able to open his eyes to see you, we don't believe he can hear anything, and it is likely that he will remain non-verbal. He also won't be able to eat without a tube. Machines are the only thing keeping him alive right now. I am so sorry... we have done everything we know possible, and there's nothing left for us to do."

He waited for a moment, but Rochelle still sat staring blankly ahead, so he continued. "Rochelle, I know this is hard to hear, but the best solution is to take him off of life support and let him go. If he somehow survives when life support is removed, we recommend you place your husband in a convalescent home. You're still so very young, and you have your precious little girl. You can go and create a new life for you and your daughter."

Rochelle asked for a moment alone with Ricardo. Then she cried out, "God, this is the test I feared so much the night I heard Ricardo share his testimony. This grief is so heavy. How will I ever do this alone? Nothing for us will ever be the same again. My pain has pulled me to a place where I can't find You. Right now, it feels like nothing good could ever come out of this. I know You brought us together to share Your love. Please give me a sign that will restore my faith and help me do the next right thing."

Rochelle sat there in traumatized silence, holding Ricardo's hand and waiting for a sign from her Heavenly Father. Then she surrendered her greatest fear of having no future with Ricardo. She told the Lord, "If it's Your will to take him home to Heaven, I will completely submit to Your sovereignty. But if You allow him to live, I promise I will care for him the rest of his life."

Then she walked out of the room with tears in her eyes and told the doctors, "Take him off life support and let the Lord decide if he lives or dies!"

Their college friends and the church youth they pastored gathered in the hospital parking lot and prayed while Ricardo was unhooked from all the machines. Miraculously, he started breathing on his own!

That day, Rochelle rededicated her life to loving Ricardo for better or for worse, in sickness and in health, just as she had promised on both of their wedding days. God knew that Rochelle's love for Ricardo would one day become a testimony of His love lived out.

Rochelle left the hospital to prepare their home to care for Ricardo there. When she returned the next day to pick him up, she wanted a sign that Ricardo knew she was there. So she decided to talk with him like he wasn't sick, and in her flirty way, said, "Ricardo, if you kiss me, I will take you home." Then she pressed her lips passionately against his. "Ricardo, please! Kiss me back, and I'll take you home."

Then she prayed, "God, let me know he can hear me and let him kiss me so that I know he can hear me. I really need this, Lord. If he can at least hear me, then I'll know my Ricardo is still in there."

Then it happened. As she kissed him one more time, he began to pucker his lips just a little to kiss her back. In that moment, she knew the doctors were wrong; Ricardo could hear! She knew even if he couldn't respond, he would at least be able to hear her voice and Clarita's. That was enough of a sign to give her the strength she needed to keep walking out her faith hand-in-hand with her Heavenly Father and her husband.

Rochelle was determined to include Ricardo in everything. Each night, she would lay little Clarita in his hospital bed in their room and read stories together as a family. Every night for nine years, she prayed for Daddy with Clarita, and then would say to their daughter, "I know Daddy's praying for you too, sweetheart." They would both kiss him goodnight. Then, once she got Clarita to sleep, she would go back into their room and press her lips passionately against Ricardo's—and every time, she could feel him try to kiss her back. Then she'd whisper in his ear, "I am so glad you're here with me!"

On Clarita's tenth birthday, Rochelle invited some friends and their children over to celebrate. Since the accident, she had only invited those she knew she could trust to support their family and respect Ricardo's dignity. Ricardo was still the love of her life, and Rochelle's biggest fear was for someone who didn't understand that to come in, see only their difficulties, and tell her she should give up on him. As a result, the only people who'd been in their home for the last decade were a few close friends and some part-time caregivers.

But today was different. Clarita had begged to invite her friends to their house and have a "normal" birthday party with everyone singing to her. Rochelle knew her daughter deserved it. She didn't want to repeat any of her mother's mistakes, even for a noble reason. So she invited all of their friends from school, church, and the community for a big tenth birthday blow-out.

Rochelle was so happy to see her daughter's face light up as their friends gathered around her and sang. But after the birthday cake was served and the kids were playing outside, Rochelle's fear became a reality: when they saw the real-life challenges Rochelle and Clarita had been facing, they began encouraging her to put Ricardo in a convalescent home and move on with her life. Rochelle explained that they didn't see Ricardo like she did. She loved him so much and was committed to caring for him—even though it was killing her not to have verbal communication with the one she loved to talk to the most, and she felt so alone.

In that moment, she decided that she needed to take Clarita to Puerto Rico and move in with Ricardo's parents for help and support. She prepared herself by learning the language. When she and Clarita arrived three months later, they were welcomed with loving arms. Ricardo's family was happy and willing to do whatever it took to care for all of them. Rochelle was especially thankful that Ricardo's father went above and beyond to be a father figure for Clarita.

Now that Clarita was ten and could read on her own, every night, she followed her mother's example and started reading her favorite stories to her daddy. Clarita knew he could hear her even though he still couldn't respond. One evening, Clarita went back into her father's room after Rochelle tucked her in bed. She was determined to have her daddy sit up and hug her; she so wanted a physical touch from him. So at ten years old, she mustered up all the faith she had and prayed, "God, please let my daddy sit up and hold me."

But when she reached over to hold his hand, she didn't feel him squeeze it back. She looked at Ricardo and said, "Daddy, sit up and hold me! I want to hug you. I want to feel you hug me back." But when she wrapped her arms around him, she felt nothing. Instead, in that moment, she felt something supernatural: invisible arms holding her as a heavenly presence and peace filled the room. With her childlike faith, she knew it was her Heavenly Daddy holding her in that very moment. Clarita could actually feel His love for her, and she never wanted to let go. She then hugged Ricardo as tightly as she could and said, "It's OK, Daddy. I know you love me, and I love you too! Goodnight!" Then she kissed him on the forehead as she did every night and ran into Rochelle's room to tell her what had happened with her Heavenly Daddy.

"Mama! Mama! God hugged me! I felt Him in Daddy's room with me!" She stopped for a second to catch her breath before continuing, "I asked Daddy for a hug, and he wanted to hug me, but he couldn't move his arms. Then I felt my Heavenly Daddy hug me. It was a really warm hug around my heart!"

Rochelle's eyes welled up with happy tears as she held her daughter tightly and began telling sweet Clarita about the night at youth group when she had felt her Heavenly Daddy hug her too—the night she gave her heart to Jesus. She was filled with renewed faith at seeing how God had touched Clarita in the same personal way He had touched her the night she became His beloved daughter.

Clarita wiped Rochelle's tears away and said, "Mama, don't worry about anything. You know our Heavenly Daddy will always be there for us." She paused for a moment, then said with a big smile, "Daddy loves us both so much. That's why he hasn't gone home to Heaven yet. He wants more time with us girls, Mama."

"Thank you, baby girl. I absolutely adore you!" Rochelle said and starting tickling her daughter. Clarita giggled and then fell asleep, tucked in with laughter and the love of her Heavenly Father.

Afterward, Rochelle went into Ricardo's room and crawled into his bed to snuggle. She meshed her hand with his hand and cried out in prayer, "Please, God, let my Ricardo feel Your love. Please help redeem this brokenness. Is there still a purpose amidst the pain? I know that You brought us together as a family, but please, God, I'm Your daughter, and I want our family to do what You sent us here to do. Please turn this trial into something beautiful. Let our testimony bless others soon!"

The Holy Spirit led her to grab Ricardo's Bible. She opened it and saw that he had highlighted Psalm 68:6: "God places the lonely in families; He sets the prisoners free and gives them joy." She knew that God had placed her in Ricardo's family, and she was so grateful for that. Now she just wanted the rest of the pieces of the puzzle of her life's purpose to come together.

Rochelle fell asleep that night holding Ricardo and his Bible. The next morning, she went downstairs and told Ricardo's mom about the highlighted scripture she had found. His mom walked to their living room, opened a dusty cabinet, reached in, and pulled out a thick leather-bound book. She put it in Rochelle's hands with tears in her eyes. "*Mira, mija... la primera pagina.*"

Rochelle saw that it was a Bible; it looked old and worn. She did as her mother-in-law told her and opened to the first page. She wept as she saw Psalm 68:6 written in Ricardo's grandma's writing on the inside of the front cover.

Ricardo's mother told Rochelle that the orphanage his grandmother had started was going to have to close because there was no one to run it. Rochelle sat there in a moment of sacred silence, in awe of God. She felt the Holy Spirit filling her heart with renewed vision. She could finally see the pieces of her purpose coming together. She once again had hope that God could turn her trials into a testimony for His glory.

Rochelle suddenly realized why she'd always had an inexplicable love for Puerto Rico—why her heart had beaten for Ricardo from the moment she first saw him, and why God did not allow his body to die. God took all the love, all the heartache, and all the trials that she had given Him over the years. She could see now how He was going to use it to continue the legacy Ricardo's grandma had started.

Rochelle got up. She had to take what she referred to as a "God walk." She needed time to reflect on the eye-opening moment. She walked down by the little stream in their village, sat on the edge, and put her feet in the water. As she watched the water rolling over her feet, she thought about how the living water of the Word of God gave her new breath that day. Then she looked down at her beautiful antique wedding ring and closed her eyes, remembering the night Ricardo had proposed to her in the park and feeling the cool breeze blow on her face as she sat there.

She realized the significance of having Ricardo's grandmother's ring. Rochelle knew now that she would continue what his grandma had started. She felt led right then to pray for her daughter's future husband the way his grandmother had prayed for her.

What Can God Do?

The next day when Clarita got home from school, Rochelle drove her to the orphanage. Clarita had a chance to meet all the kids who didn't have a mommy or a daddy here on Earth, but who had joy in their hearts knowing they were children of God and that they were not fatherless. As a matter of fact, the name of the orphanage was "His Royal Family."

Later on the way home, Clarita said, "Mama, we need to go visit every day."

Rochelle responded by testing what God put on her heart. "Honey, what do you think about helping run the orphanage?"

Clarita was ecstatic. "Yes, Mama! Let's go to the orphanage every day with the kids and be their spiritual family!"

Rochelle knew Ricardo's mom would help care for him during the day. She smiled at the thought that they were doing what Ricardo would have done to carry on his grandma's legacy. Though he could not say it, the girls knew he was proud of them. Every evening when they came home, they'd sit by his bed and tell him their God stories from the day and how they helped the orphans learn more about being children of the King!

Ten more years passed; Clarita turned twenty. She married the man Rochelle had prayed for; he was a local pastor whom she absolutely adored. They met at the orphanage, where his church volunteered every week.

Rochelle was determined that Ricardo would attend their daughter's wedding. His father brought him in a wheelchair with full body support. Even though Ricardo couldn't open his eyes to see the ceremony, Rochelle knew he could feel the love of family. At the reception, Clarita gave a speech about her father, her grandfather, and her Heavenly Father. She shared how blessed she felt to get to honor three fathers at her wedding, and it made an everlasting impact on all who were there. Rochelle held Ricardo's hand after the speech and leaned over to him, saying, "Honey, this is what God can do when we see our lives through Heaven's eyes." She felt Ricardo squeeze her hand, and she knew in her heart that she had done the right thing.

A few weeks later, Ricardo's health suddenly declined. On the day he went home to be with the Lord, Rochelle, Clarita, and both of his parents prayed together. They asked their Heavenly Father if He would open Ricardo's eyes so he could see them one last time before he passed into eternity. God answered, and right before he took his last breath, Ricardo opened his eyes and looked at both of his girls for the first and last time since his accident.

They all cried together, yet they had peace in knowing Ricardo was finally truly living.

Two years after he passed, Clarita and her husband had their first baby. It was a boy, and they named him Ricardo.

WHAT CAN I DO?

Care for Your Loved Ones

Rochelle knew that leaving Ricardo without family, alone in a convalescent home, was heartbreaking and wrong. I know it's hard to care for those who can't care for themselves, but it's probably the most important ministry you'll ever have. Honor your parents by taking care of them and take care of your loved ones the way you would want to be cared for if you were in that position.

Use Your Pain for Purpose

Rochelle spent the rest of her life traveling the world and sharing her testimony to raise money for the orphanage. Every time she spoke, she let the world know that Jesus gave up everything for her, so she was more than happy to give up everything for Him. Scripture says, "Those who lose their life will find it"—and when

Rochelle lost the life she loved in that car accident, she found God's ultimate purpose for her. She holds on to the hope that one day in Heaven, she will get to hold her Ricardo, hear his voice, and spend eternity celebrating the work that was done on Earth for the Kingdom of God.

His Love Letter to You

You are my precious daughter.

You are a daughter of the King, and not just any king. You are My daughter, and I am the God of all Heaven and Earth. I'm delighted with you! You are the apple of My eye. You're Daddy's girl. Your earthly father may love and adore you, but his love is not perfect, no matter how great—or small—it is. Only My love is perfect...because I am Love. I formed your body. I fashioned your mind and soul. I know your personality; I understand your needs and desires. I see your heartaches and disappointments, and I love you passionately and patiently. My child, I bought you with a price so that we could have an intimate relationship for all eternity. Soon we will see each other face-to-face—Father and daughter—and you will experience the wonderful place I have prepared for you in Paradise. Until then, fix your eyes on Heaven and walk closely with Me. You will know that—although I am God—My arms are not too big to hold you.

Love,

Your King and Daddy in Heaven

"You didn't choose me, I chose you." (John 15:16)

Chapter 9

BEYOND HERE AND NOW

GOD, HELP ME LOVE AND LIVE DRIVEN BY ETERNITY UNTIL YOU RETURN FOR ME ONE DAY.

"And I saw the holy city, the new Jerusalem, coming down from God out of heaven like a bride beautifully dressed for her husband."
Revelation 21:2

I know it's hard to imagine what it will be like on the day the Lord returns for His bride, and I know there is a descriptive biblical illustration in 1 Peter. However, I pray that this allegory God gave me will paint a beautiful picture of what it will feel like if we're ready when the Lord returns to get us, and I hope the romantic in you can thoroughly enjoy dreaming of that day as you read this story written for you, His bride...

His bride-to-be stood motionless, staring in the mirror for what seemed like an eternity. Her hair and makeup were works of art, and her dress was beyond stunning. Never before had she felt so perfectly beautiful. But something in her did not feel right or ready for her prince.

She couldn't figure out why, on her most glorious day in time, her state of mind was totally unsettled. As she continued to look at herself in the mirror, she could not help but reflect on the way she had loved and lived her life leading up to this day.

She knew her prince loved her, and she dreamed about the day he would return for her. But she was sad to realize that, when she glanced at her daily "to do" list, there was nothing on it about this promised day.

She felt so embarrassed that she hadn't shared about the love of her life, the one who was coming to rescue her. She was disappointed in herself. How had she forgotten to hand out the beautiful invitations to her guests for their wedding feast? She glanced over at her open guest book, but every page was blank.

She couldn't believe what was happening. What should have been the most magnificent day of her life was turning into a day of regret. Tears ran down her perfectly made-up face. She couldn't look at herself any longer because of her shame. When she looked away from the mirror, she noticed a huge pile of letters in a beautiful box with her name on it.

The bride fumbled through the stacks of unopened letters. Every one was addressed to her. Each had been sent from the same person—her beloved prince. He longed to connect with her, so he sent her love letters every day, leading all the way up to this divinely designed day.

Tears blurred her vision, then the heaviness of her heart began to lighten up, and her eyes brightened as she read the sweet, loving words her prince had written on one of the envelopes: "I can't wait to see you, my beloved bride. I am preparing a place for you right now and will be there soon to bring you here."

A sense of excitement and eagerness overcame her soul as she opened the envelope. Just then, she heard the most majestic music she had ever heard. It filled the bridal room. Her spirit soared as she knew the wedding march had begun!

She took one last look in the mirror to fix her veil, then ran with anticipation toward the large jeweled double doors. The doors swung open, revealing the most breathtaking sanctuary she could have imagined. She gathered herself, took a deep breath, and started marching down the aisle, her eyes dancing about to absorb the indescribable beauty of her surroundings.

It was the most beautiful, bittersweet moment she had ever experienced. She couldn't believe how blessed she was to be there. But she still felt heartbroken that she hadn't invited the people she knew and loved. She realized that fear of their rejection had kept her from reaching out to invite them. She couldn't wait to see her prince face-to-face, but she so wished that those she knew were there with her to witness this moment. She began to feel unworthy because she had left so much Kingdom work undone.

Then suddenly, everything around her seemed to blur as she caught sight of him. He looked so tender and loving, standing there at the end of the aisle. His smile was inviting as he patiently waited for his bride to approach. There were no bridesmaids or groomsmen—only her groom and what appeared to be stacks and stacks of wedding presents.

She had heard that her prince had prepared many gifts for her, but this was truly overwhelming. She had always known her emotions would run wild on her eternal wedding day, but nothing had prepared her for the intense flood of feelings that filled her heart. As she approached her groom—her prince—she felt his heart for her. But her face grew flushed with shame and embarrassment. It suddenly hit her, like a stabbing jolt of reality: He had done everything to prepare for this day. He had done everything to woo her, to bless her, to capture her heart, to rescue her . . . and she had done nothing! She had nothing to offer Him: no gifts, no guests. She had loved and labored for all the wrong things and for all the wrong reasons.

The depth of her shame grew so intense that she grabbed the hem of her gown and turned, ready to run away. Then she heard his calm, compassionate voice say, "Don't run, my beloved!" She slowly turned back and reluctantly continued to walk toward him. Her eyes met his, and she saw something in his gaze that was more intense than her shame, more powerful than her sorrow. That "something" was greater than anything she had ever experienced. Something shifted in her soul. Something supernatural was happening as he extended his hand to her and helped her

> up the steps to stand next to him. She was mesmerized by this moment and captivated by how he looked into her eyes.
>
> As their eyes locked, her shame began to melt away. She pressed in closer to him, never breaking eye contact. Now that she could see it, the look on his face was one of pure, unconditional love for her. She had never known this kind of love existed. As she surrendered to this surreal moment, every negative emotion loosed its grip on her and departed forever. Every pain that had burrowed its way into her soul disappeared for good. The prince extended his hand to hold her close. Then he sweetly smiled at her and gently wiped the tears from her cheek.
>
> He embraced His new bride and said, "You will never cry again, my love. Welcome to the home I have prepared for you."

If you know Jesus as your Savior, then He is your Prince, and you are His princess. This story is about your glorious day. However, the end of this story and the fruits of that day are up to you, His bride-to-be. There's so much He has for you! It's such a privilege to be His princess and His bride. I pray that the rest of the teaching in this chapter will inspire you to get ready for the greatest day the world will ever know—your eternal wedding day, the day when your Prince, Jesus, comes for you, His bride!

What Can God Do?

In this chapter, I'm not going break down a list of what God can do because He already did it all when He sent His Son to die for our sins. It's unimaginable that He would take His only Son and punish Him for what we did wrong, then reward us with eternity. Over the past five years, as my life has been dismantled in every way, I kept reminding myself that what Jesus did on the cross for me was enough for me to continue to follow Him for better or for worse. So in this chapter, I will lead you in a prayer I said to Him in my darkest hour.

Wedding Vows to Your Prince Jesus

DEAR JESUS,

I take You as my EVERLASTING LORD and PRINCE, loving what I know of You, and TRUSTING what I do not yet know.

I take You, Jesus, for BETTER or for WORSE, for RICHER or for POORER, in times of SICKNESS and in times of HEALTH, in times of JOY and in times of SORROW, in times of FAILURE and in times of TRIUMPH, in times of PLENTY and in times of WANT.

Today, I give You, JESUS, all my HEART to HAVE and to HOLD until YOU RETURN or until death places me in Your arms forever.

Love,

Your Princess Bride who says "I DO"

WHAT CAN I DO?

God can do anything if we give Him a chance. He says nothing is impossible for Him, and He promises that if you give your life to Him, He will give you back a life that actually makes a difference in this world. I want you to take a moment with this last chapter to journal all the things you can think of that He's already done for you personally. When you've done that, meditate on those things.

Once you've meditated on those things, celebrate them and feast on His faithfulness from this day forward.

Love God with Your Whole Heart

> And you must love the Lord your God with all your heart, all your soul, all your mind, and all your strength. (Mark 12:30)

Jesus says this is the first and the greatest commandment. He wants your heart more than He wants anything else. He knows that your heart is safe in His hands. He also says to guard your heart because it is the wellspring of your life. He is the safest place for you to surrender your heart and the only way to protect it.

Represent Him with Humility

Humility is the most beautiful thing ever to God. He says, "I will lift up the humble." He loves when you're humble because He loves to lift you up. He longs to trust you with great and mighty things here on Earth, but He can only give His great gifts to the humble.

> So humble yourselves under the mighty power of God, and at the right time He will lift you up in honor. (1 Peter 5:6)

Represent Him with Your Pure Holiness

The only way for us to set ourselves apart is with purity and holiness. We are divine diplomats and daughters of the Most High King. The more we respect ourselves enough to remain pure, the more others will want to hear what we have to say about the King. You are too special to give away what is sacred any longer. Treat yourself to God's gift of holiness and purify yourself so He can do great and mighty things through you.

> God's will is for you to be holy, so stay away from all sexual sin. Then each of you will control his own body and live in holiness and honor.... (1 Thessalonians 4:3–4)

Represent Him with Honor

When we really recognize who God is and who we are, we begin to realize what an honor it is to be part of the royal family. Be careful not to let anybody dishonor you and don't dishonor others just because you disagree with them. You can always choose to represent your King by acting and reacting honorably. Make it your mission to reflect who you are in Christ. Also, remember that people who dishonor you are not true friends. When at all possible, surround yourself with people who honor you and be sure that you honor them in return. In doing so, you will create an atmosphere that is beautiful and can flourish.

Even Jesus could not perform miracles in His own family when they dishonored him. When you walk into a room, whether it's your home or a friend's, remember to walk with honor and to treat others with honor. Don't connect your heart to people who dishonor you. I know sometimes those people are in your family and that there's no way of getting away from them, but purpose yourself not to allow their dishonor to define you. Don't let their dishonor stop you from acting with honor. You're a child of the King; you're the bride of Christ.

Represent Him with Love for Humanity

I know there's a lot in the world to be angry about. It's easy to begin to develop anger toward humanity when you no longer feel love for them. But remember that God tells us to love our neighbors as we love ourselves. He also tells us to love our enemies. Don't let the hate you have for someone's actions make you hate humanity. You are here to reflect God's love, so guard your heart from hate.

> Dear friends, let us continue to love one another, for love comes from God. Anyone who loves is a child of God and knows God. But anyone who does not love does not know God, for God is love. (1 John 4:7–8)

WHAT'S THE TRUTH?

The Truth Is This Is Not Our Home

When you are overwhelmed by the things you see in this world, remember that this is not your forever home. You are a citizen of Heaven! You are here to represent Heaven on Earth. Don't let the things of this world keep you from representing the things of Heaven. Remember who you are and represent Him well. Take as many people home with you to Heaven as possible. That is your royal responsibility to our King. We came into this world with nothing, and that's how we will leave. We can't take anything with us except what we did for eternity.

The Truth Is It's about Our Character, Not Our Appearance

So many times, we put all our effort into our appearance—and not just our physical appearance, but the appearance of how we seem to others. It is always best for you to walk in the example of Christ in order to work on your character. Look at what God did for Job as he continued to walk in character and integrity. God returned to him twice as much as he had lost. Look at what God did with Joseph as he continued to walk in character and integrity. He took him out of prison and put him in charge of a nation.

When it's all said and done, the image we try to project is powerless. But our character is a perfect way to represent ourselves and our God. Our character will be an example to guide our children.

The Truth Is It's about Our Choices, Not Our Possessions

God says to us today, "I give you a choice between life and death, between blessing and curses." He says, "I call on Heaven and Earth that you would choose life." God has so many riches for us when we choose life. These riches will be waiting for us in Heaven and celebrated for all eternity. Don't trade the riches of Heaven to get rich on Earth. It's wonderful if you can make a great living, as long as you are generous and use it for God's causes. But if it becomes your identity, then you've lost the only treasure that really matters—who you are in Christ. Who we are in Christ is the only identity that will live long after we have left this earth.

The Truth Is It's about Our Compassion, Not Our Comfort

Compassion is the most beautiful gift you can give a friend or loved one who is desperate. God's people, filled with compassion, can change the world one person at a time.

HIS LOVE LETTER TO YOU

My Beloved,

I want to reveal a sacred secret to you, My Beloved. Although I am your God, I am also your Eternal Husband. I will come soon to carry you over the threshold into eternity. My desire is to lift the veil from your eyes so that you might see who you really are, My Princess, My Bride. The time is now, My beloved Bride, to get ready for My return. I will come quickly for you, and in that moment, you will be changed. I want you to live as if there were no tomorrow. I want your heart and mind fixed on eternity with Me. If you will do as I request, you will be ready for Me when I come. I promise you this, Princess: nothing here on earth is everlasting but My love for you. Now, let Me dress you in humility and robe you in righteousness until I walk you down the aisle of eternity.

Love,

Your Eternal Husband

"Let us be glad and rejoice, and let us give honor to him. For the time has come for the wedding feast of the Lamb, and his bride has prepared herself." (Revelation 19:7)

HIS PROMISES TO YOU, HIS BELOVED:

There will be a new heaven and a new earth, for the old heaven and the old earth have disappeared. And the sea is also gone. And there will be a holy city, the new Jerusalem, coming down from God out of heaven like a bride beautifully dressed for her husband. (Revelation 21:1–2)

"He will wipe every tear from their eyes, and there will be no more death or sorrow or crying or pain. All these things are gone forever." And the one sitting on the throne said, "Look, I am making everything new!" And then he said to me, "Write this down, for what I tell you is trustworthy and true." (Revelation 21:4–6)

It is finished! I am the Alpha and the Omega—the Beginning and the End. To all who are thirsty I will give freely from the springs of the water of life. All who are victorious will inherit all these blessings, and I will be their God, and they will be my children. (Revelation 21:6–7)

AFTERWORD

As we come to the close of our time together in this book, I'd like to recap the life lessons from each chapter that I pray would stay with you from this day forward as you walk out your faith...

CHAPTER 1: BEYOND BETRAYAL

Revenge Only Feels Good for a Moment

You're part of the royal family, a divine diplomat, and you will always win by keeping your integrity with a right reaction that will last a lifetime.

Exchange Bitterness for a Better Outcome

Never become like those who have hurt you. Be the bigger person and get a better outcome.

Do the Next Right Thing

I know how hard it is when you're hurting to do the right thing, but it will be the one thing you never regret.

CHAPTER 2: BEYOND FORGIVENESS

There Is a Difference between a Bitter Heart and a Broken Heart

A bitter heart wants revenge and will not release the past until they get it. A broken heart wants healing and help from God so it can move on.

Toxic Love Is Not God

Toxic love will make your heart sick; healthy love will make your heart soar.

Set Healing Boundaries

If those boundaries are not respected, there must be a temporary or complete break from the relationship.

CHAPTER 3: BEYOND SHATTERED

Let the Tears Fall

Tears will go much further than talking about the pain over and over again. God's truth and your tears will begin healing your broken heart.

Stay Close to God

Many times when grief happens, especially in death, we walk away from the only One who can heal and help us.

Get Real with God

Feelings of guilt, anger, despair, and fear—let me reassure you that what you feel is normal. Don't judge yourself or others if you're helping someone through grief.

CHAPTER 4: BEYOND SHAME

God Does Not Remember Your Sin

God says He forgets our sins and remembers them no more. However, He allows us to remember our mistakes so we don't repeat them. Then we can help others find their way to forgiveness.

Repentance Is a Gift

Repenting is a safe way to get naked before God and allow Him to compassionately cleanse your soul of all secret sins and shame.

There Is a Difference between Shame and Being Ashamed

Shame is a set-up from Satan to keep you down. Knowing what you did was wrong will keep you humble.

God Gives Second Chances

You can mourn and learn from your mistakes, and that's healthy. You can accept the consequences of your mistakes, and that's maturity. But when you deny yourself the grace of God to move forward, that's bondage.

Chapter 5: Beyond Motherhood

Give God Your Dream

One good question to ask yourself if you're disappointed is whether your dream would have blessed anybody else's life besides yours.

Filter Your Feelings

Remember your feelings are different every day, and you cannot use them to filter your faith. When you're in a season of suffering, hang on to the Word of God and the truth that every season of suffering has an expiration date.

Listen for God's Voice

God's voice is a peaceful knowing, not a desperate wanting. God's voice is always confirmed in His Word, not in our worries.

CHAPTER 6: BEYOND SICKNESS AND DISEASE

Today Is All You Have

We need to live every day as if it's our last because one day we're going to be right. Death is the door that leads to a beautiful, everlasting eternity.

Sickness Is Not God's Will

The fact is that we live in a toxic world, we eat toxic food, we have toxic stress, and very rarely do we take care of God's temple, our bodies. However, God can use sickness for His Kingdom to be furthered on Earth through us.

Death Is Not the End

It is appointed to man to die but once, and God will decide that day. However, death is actually the beginning, and Eternity is the only life that will matter when it's all said and done.

CHAPTER 7: BEYOND TEMPTATION

God's Grace Is Greater Than Our Mistake

There is a price to pay when we fall and sin against God. However, the same God who disciplines us because He loves us also sent us a Savior to give us the power to get up and fight for our faith.

God Is Not Mad at You

He is for you, and if you've blown it, He wants to help you get back up again. He wants to compassionately help you through the consequences of your sin.

Get Accountability

No matter how much you love Jesus, and no matter how much you have good intentions, you're still human—you need accountability, and so do I. This life was not meant to be done alone. Get yourself in a small group and be transparent.

Chapter 8: Beyond Fatherlessness

You're a Daughter of the King

You are a daughter of the King, and not just any king. You are His chosen daughter, and He is delighted with you! You are the apple of His eye. You're Daddy's girl.

Your Heavenly Father Knows You

He formed your body. He fashioned your mind and soul. He knows your personality, and He understands your needs and desires. He wants you to let Him care for you. And He will meet your need to feel loved.

Remember Your Father's Faithfulness

When you're going through pain, purpose yourself to remember His faithfulness in the past. Practicing this will give you peace in the present, knowing that He will be faithful again.

Chapter 9: Beyond Here and Now

The Gift of Salvation

There's no way I could close out this chapter without inviting you to receive Christ as your Savior. It's not an accident that you're reading this book. Maybe you've been to church, or maybe your grandparents are Christians, but God is inviting you right now to have a personal relationship with Him and a place in Heaven by receiving His son, Jesus Christ, into your heart. If that is you, I invite you to pray and repeat this prayer out loud and believe it in your heart, and you will be saved.

Salvation Prayer

Dear Jesus, I believe You died on the cross for me, and I ask You to forgive me of my sins and everything I've ever done wrong against You. I invite You now to come into my heart, and I commit to make You the Lord of my life. I pray this prayer by faith in Your name, amen.

Eternal Perspective

When it's all said and done, when this life is over and we are in eternity looking back at our life on Earth, we will find that the only thing that matters is what we did to prepare for eternity.

If I never meet you here on Earth, I look forward to celebrating with you in Heaven. Until then, I pray that you fight the good fight, keep your faith, and finish strong!

Love,

Sheri Rose

ACKNOWLEDGMENTS

I have to take a moment to acknowledge the beautiful people that God gifted me with for this book to become reality.

Tim Peterson: I'm thankful that you're not only my publisher, but you've also become a brother. I am beyond blessed to have worked with you on this project!

To Jennifer, my marketing girl: Thank you for your amazing input and helping me put a bow on this book.

To my editor, Christianne Gillespie: It's hard to find words to express my deep appreciation for you. First of all, I'm in awe that you were able to do anything, much less edit this entire book, while homeschooling four kids ages three to ten in the midst of quarantine. I'm like having ten kids when you work with me on a book! Christianne, to be honest, this project would not have happened without your beautiful heart and your wisdom to see things I would have missed.

To my cheerleaders:

I adore my faithful and fun friends: Heidi, Renee, Barb, Teri, Chelsea, Shawn, Anna, Karen, Kari, Judy, and Jodie. Thank you for your priceless prayers, for picking me up when I wanted to quit, for sharing my pain, and for helping me push through the harder days. You girls took the time to talk through and bring clarity to all the stories.

To my spiritual parents, Poppy and my angel LeeAnn: Thank you for sharing your wisdom and your wonderful love of family as I visited the pain from my past in writing this book.

To my daddy, Phil Goodman, who has always believed in me even when I didn't believe in myself: I am beyond blessed to be your daughter. I can't imagine who I'd be without you to speak life into me every day.

To Karen Kingsbury: Thank you for believing in me enough to endorse this book!

Last but not least, to my daughter Emmy Joy: You have become my very best friend and the most extraordinary person I know on the earth! Thank you for believing in your mama, baby girl!

Love,

Sheri Rose